The **NEW** Energy Anatomy

Nine new views of human energy

That don't require any clairvoyance!

The easy way to learn about energy!

:=:=+=:=:=+=:=:=+=:=:=+=:

Bruce Dickson ~ Healing Toolbox

The NEW Energy Anatomy

Nine new views of how human energy is organized;

The easiest way to learn about human energy.

No clairvoyance required!

ISBN-13: 978-1456517557

ISBN-10: 1456517554

Author: Bruce Dickson

Published by Bruce Dickson

Book Design by Petru Dumitru

Copyright 2011 Bruce Dickson

Other publisher inquiries welcome

\v\V/v/

Tools That Heal Press

www.HealingToolbox.org

All books below available in paper and eBook. All written with humor and insight by a practicing Health Intuitive.

- ***Your Habit Body, An Owner's Manual*** Our habits are our best friends; why then, do we make the same errors over and over again?

- ***Self-Healing 101,*** Nine Experiments in Self-healing You Can Do at Home to Awaken the Inner Healer

- ***Meridian Metaphors,*** *Psychology of the Meridians and Major Organs*

- "***Willingness to heal*** is the pre-requisite for all healing"

- ***You Have Three Selves Vol. ONE***; Simply the clearest model of the whole person; Orientation

- ***You Have Three Selves; Vol. TWO*** Simply the clearest model of the whole person, Find the 3S in your life & pop culture

- ***The Inner Court***: Close-up of the Habit Body

- ***The NEW Energy Anatomy***: Nine new views of human energy; No clairvoyance required.

- **Radical Cell Wellness—Especially for women!**
Cell psychology for everyone; A coherent theory of illness and wellness

- **The Five Puberties**, Growing new eyes to see children afresh

- **How We Heal; and, Why do we get sick?**
Including 35 better, more precise questions on wellness and healing, answered by a Medical Intuitive

- **You have FIVE bodies PACME**; Spiritual Geography 101

- **The Meaning of Illness is Now an Open Book**, Cross-referencing illness and issues

- **Rudolf Steiner's Fifth Gospel in Story Form**
Topics include the TWO Jesus children and the active participation of the Buddha in the Christ event.

Longer book descriptions at end of this book

To Learn More:

http://HealingToolbox.org

http://wholistic.theholisticchamberofcommerce.com

HealingToolbox.org ~ 310-280-1176

Bruce also recommends www.MSIA.org It helped me put myself back together again.

The best solution is always loving

If you get stuck, give me a call.

Table of Contents

Armor of the Spiritual Warrior, slightly updated 1
Why not start here? 3
The easier starting place for understanding auras-chakras-meridians 4
   Short version of your own Energy Anatomy: Inner Dashboard 9
     How to navigate a range of frequency 9
     What was wrong with auras, chakras and meridians?. 10
     Why human energy anatomy? 11
     Identify all the primary causative factors 12
     Why can't it all be One? 14
     The Law of Rumi 14
     The paradox of mapping a hologram 15
     Where did this stuff come from? 16
     How to make your aura brighter 19
     Q: How energetic anatomy differs from physical anatomy 20
     Q: Do I need to be clairvoyant to use this? 20
     Q: Why New Energy Anatomy NOW? 20

The human psyche as One Whole and first distinctions 23
     What is One Whole in human energy? 23
     The first obvious distinction: range of frequency 23
     The second obvious distinction: north and south 23
     Range and "choice" 24

You have three levels of creativity 26
     What's down there in my unconscious? 26
     We have three levels of creativity and responsibility .. 27

Conscious creativity characterized 28
Sub-conscious creativity 28
Unconscious creativity 29
We have issues on three levels of creativity 31
Three levels as words-feeling-needs 33
Using self-testing to navigate our issues 33
Waking, Dreaming and Sleeping 34
Pretty good definition of maturity 35
Waking, dreaming, sleeping in cell physiology 35
How deep is my issue? The iceberg metaphor 36
Peeling the artichoke 38
Language is leverage 39
Personal responsibility on three frequency levels 39
Ask your worst enemy what's wrong with you 40
Our issues are like a game of pick-up-sticks 41
Two great questions to begin all your sessions with ... 42
Example of being of two minds 43
Undercharged or overcharged? 45
Towards a theory of under and overcharge 45
Metaphors for under- and over charge 46
A theory of undercharge 47
A theory of balance 47
Defining some terms 47
Check Willingness to Heal SECOND 48
The Law of Gentleness for practitioners 49
The Law of Gentleness asks only one question 51
How to avoid a healing crisis 52
First three etheric centers = your physical body 52

NINE NEW VIEWS 54
~ View ONE ~ 54

v

Right & left sides of the body, The magic of YANG & *Yin* 54
    Dogs and cats as a fresh entry point to YANG~*yin* 56
    YANG & yin for modern minds, three views 57
    Consider a baby chick exiting its egg 57
    Consider Grail and Sword 57
    The etheric body as yin container, the astral body as active YANG 58
    Consider the yin-YANG symbol 58
    Right and Left in English and Spanish 61
    Right and Left as boy and girl numbers....................... 61
    Right and Left as digestion and assimilation 62
    Our two nervous systems play out R~L 64
    Your rational mind can be either thinking or feeling ... 65
    R~L as "love" (active) and "be loved" (receptive) 66
    R~L as masculine and feminine approaches 67
    R~L as fight and flight 68
    Seeing YANG and yin in your own body: 68
    R~L: Bogart & Bergman in "Casablanca" 68
    R~L: Harold Hill & Marion the Librarian in The Music Man 69
    Our right side is our Arnold Schwarzenegger side 70
    Ingrid Bergman & Judy Garland are our left side 71
    Isn't this just Kidney YANG, kidney yin? 72
    RIGHT sided YANG expressions 72
    LEFT sided yin expressions 72
    Healthy Yin as "the still small voice within" 73
    Healthy Yin is not "passive" and not "surrender" 73
    YANG~*yin* as healthy push~pull 74
    Punch & Judy puppets as "liver attacking pancreas-spleen" in TCM 76

Punch & Judy puppets as modern negative self-talk	77
R~L sides and altered states	77
Our body is most polarized lower	78
Our weak left-sided personal boundaries	79
R~L as two halves of "self-confidence"	79
R~L as goals-projects~needs	80
R~L sides as father & mother issues	81
Right~Left as inner father and inner mother	82
R~L sides as how we face the 3D world	83
R~L hip & leg contrast	84
Question for self-study R~L	84
R~L as two halves of abundance & prosperity	85
Abundance on the right side feels like this	85
Abundance on the left side feels like this	85
R~L as "firing on both cylinders"	87
R~L as younger and old in the our psyche	87
R~L as lion & lamb	88
R~L as two halves of seeing	88
R~L as healthy "yes" and healthy "no"	88
R~L as two halves of receptivity	89
Much more on R~L in Heart Psychology	89
Our body heals from right to left	90
Strokes and R~L imbalances	91
When R~L are mixed up: mixed dominance	91
Our culture is out of whack RIGHT~*left*	92
A caricature of RIGHT~*left*	93
R~L as the two fears of the psoas muscles	93
R~L as two different upward spirals	94
R~L as goals and needs	95
We have goals on our right side	95

Needs are on our left side 95
English language tracks us towards goals 96
Dreams as needs 96
Wants or needs?... 97
A way to clarify your fulfillment needs 97
Needs PACMES 98
We can be split-off from our needs by "towards" and "away" 99
FAQs... 100
Needs are primarily inner experiences 101
Final words on R~L 102
Summary of R~L 102
The Prayer of right and left 103

~ New view TWO ~ 104

The human hourglass...104

Caroline Myss' hourglass image 105
Different tempos above and below 105
Enteric and Cerebral Nervous systems (NS)............... 107
ENS-CNS as self-esteem and self-concept.................. 109
One nervous system dominates in the adult hourglass
.... 110
Loving and feeling connect top and bottom 110
You have two minds and this is a good thing............. 111
Objections to "the human psyche has two poles" 112
The human cell has magnetic poles 112
Preferences Right~Left, Top~Bottom 114
Top and bottom as see-saw, as teeter-totter 115
Top and bottom as "heat rises"................................... 117
Our body heals from top to bottom........................... 118

~ New view THREE ~ 119

Earthly human energy is organized front and back 119
    Front of body: Magnetism ~ Back of body: Electricity 119
        Feeling and willingness ~ Character and strength 120
        Front of body > CV > Clark Kent the weakling 121
        Back of body > GV > muscle-bound Superman in action 122
        Superman and Clark Kent 122

~ New view FOUR ~ 125
Laughter as anatomy lesson 125
    The four colors of the spectrum of laughter 128
    Four laughters as measures of inner teamwork R~L .. 129

~ New view FIVE ~ 131
Our gut brain is organized top and bottom 131
    "Feeling-desire" is the frequency of the subconscious 132

~ New view SIX ~ 134
Our gut brain has four quadrants 134
    Bertrand Babinet's Inner Family in the gut 135
    Which family archetype do you play the most? 137
    Inner Family members briefly characterized 137
    Inner Court members related to physical anatomy ... 138
    Inner Court as William Glasser's Five Human Needs . 139
    GLMA as Supporter, Promoter, Analyzer, Controller .. 140
    The most visual model of the human psyche 141
    Which Inner Court archetype are you most like? 142
    Right and left side "teams" in the solar plexus 145
    Is my b/s male or female? 146
    R~L sides of our bodies as younger and older 147

~ New view SEVEN ~ 149
Four quadrants of our head brain 149
    The c/s is turned 90 degrees from the b/s 149
    Right rear brain: Guinever 152
    Arthur, front left, is General George Patton 152
    Lancelot, front right, is James Thurber 153
    Fifth element in the head? 153
    Our human brain wakes up and develops from back to front 154
    Rear brain quadrants as J~P in MBTI 154
    The four brain quadrants in self-healing 155
    The four quadrants of the body 156
    How Inner Court in the head affects Inner Court in the gut 157
    Speculation on other arrangements 157
    RIGHT~left converged with Inner Court 158

~ New view EIGHT ~ 160
Back of our head: willingness to heal our own past 160
    Axis of function in the back of the head 160
    In the healthy walled city 161
    Overcharge and undercharge in back of the head..... 162

~ New view NINE ~ 163
Our hip girdle as a Ring of Loving 163
    Hip and neck problems as energetic instability 163
    Four issues in more modern terms 165
    Four spheres of relationship in the 3D world 166
    My Ring of Loving, where is it weak? 168

Lining up for success   RIGHT~*left* in the body ... 170

Intro to the Three Selves The nature of human nature Simply the clearest model of the whole person 172
    Three Selves & the Inner Court 172

To Learn More 175
    Handy map of Creation, Spiritual Geography PACME, short version 175
    Spiritual Geography from low frequency to high........ 176
    PACME detail ~ low frequency to high frequency...... 176
    PACME can also be concentric circles 180
    What's above Creation? 180
    Our Many Selves... 182

Check willingness to heal FIRST for practitioners 183
    One practitioner's dilemma 183
    How I used to do sessions 184
    Case study: How I do sessions now............................. 184

When coaching does not work: check depth of issue 186

How to make your aura brighter 187
    Energetic strength 188

Make your cells brighter 191

Why auras and seven chakras are naturally the tail, not the dog of energy anatomy 192
    Our 'habit body' as a 'habit hologram' 193

About the Author 199

Tools That Heal Press booklist 200

Best Selling titles 201

Connect with the Author ~ 226

Sessions with the author 227
Training with the Author..228
Reading Group Guide 229
Other CLASSICS of self-healing & Medical Intuition
....230

Armor of the Spiritual Warrior, slightly updated

It's fun to say I learned how to think from Rudolf Steiner and I learned how to love from John-Roger.

Part of my education in loving is J-R's qualities of the spiritual warrior. His version is:

>Health, wealth and happiness;

Loving, caring and sharing;

>Abundance, prosperity, and riches; and

>Touching to others with all of our gifts.

I find these lovely percepts to live by and to work with in self-healing sessions. At PTS.org you can find a book, class locations and email courses on Spiritual Warrior.

I've found an additional distinction. It has been fruitful both for me and for clients. "Touching to others with all of our gifts, all of our goodness" addresses our YANG function, on the right side of our body.

What about the left side, our yin side?

The word level might go like this, "Allowing others to touch to us with all of their goodness."

Q: Wait! Are we inviting anyone, everyone, to touch to us anytime, any where?

A: Nosiree, Bob. Tho awkward and unpoetic in English, what seems to work is this:

Allowing others to touch to us with all of their goodness

NEW Energy Anatomy

Keeping clear, our mutually healthy boundaries.

This new distinction has assisted me and my clients to increase healthy receptivity (kidney yin, left side). It also points to our need to allow and promote money and abundance finding us, recognizing us, flowing into and towards us.

This expands the Armor of the Spiritual Warrior to:

Health, wealth and happiness;

Loving, caring and sharing;

Abundance, prosperity and riches; and

Touching to others with all of our gifts.

Allowing others to touch to us with all of their goodness;

Keeping clear, our mutually healthy boundaries.

If you find more useful distinctions about the armor of the Spiritual Warrior, I'd enjoy hearing them.

The armor of the Spiritual Warrior is, in a word, happiness.

v\V/v

Why not start here?

Tho invisible, the human psyche need not be mysterious. Basic practical and useful distinctions in human energy are perceptible and verifiable with muscle testing of any kind.

'Each person heals somewhat uniquely,' is still true. While muscle testing works primarily in the domain of one person, it can be used to verify and validate the basic "landmarks" in human energy.

Q: Is this the same as NLP Metaprograms?

A: No, but they do overlap. The endgame of NLP is largely about perceiving and recognizing patterns in our sub- and unconscious. NEW Energy Anatomy is more about structures, even tho they are invisible to most of us. The dividing line between where structures leave off and patterns begin should be more obvious after reading this book.

This is also NOT like your mother's and father's old chakra books.

Animal anatomy makes useful distinctions within meat, bone and tissues. Plant anatomy makes useful distinctions between cells and functions. Using muscle testing of any kind, NEW Energy Anatomy makes useful distinctions in the structure and frequencies of invisible human psyches.

The most natural divisions-distinctions in our human psyche

Better than auras-chakras-meridians, once you can muscle test, it turns out the older, simpler organizing ideas of top~bottom, right~left, front~back and classic sagital, coronal planes serve much better for locating

NEW Energy Anatomy

invisible disturbances.

The easier starting place for understanding auras-chakras-meridians

Visible anatomy, our own familiar body image, and simple compass directions, comprise a better starting place for locating invisible disturbances than auras-chakras-meridians.

Q: Why?

A: Because your anatomy and 3D directional tools are ten times more familiar! You have experienced your body and a compass and directions. Most of us have little to no direct perception of auras-chakras-meridians.

Q: This sounds too obvious. So what?

A: Two "so-whats." One is what you are looking for in self-healing is almost always going to be invisible. It makes sense to use tools you re most confident with to find things never seen before.

The other "so-what" is as Earth's frequency continues to rise, we are all becoming less and less embodied. Using our body image supports us staying grounded when working with invisible targets in self-healing. It also support us working smart, not hard: use simple locational tools already at hand before you get creative. You will have plenty of opportunity for creativity. Rest up for when you need it. Until then stick with location-location-location until that runs out.

TFT-EFT, meridian tapping, took off and became big in the 1990s. The Innerwise.eu healing system appears poised to take off and become big publicly for similar reasons. Each of these is effective; none require expensive expert training. With any of these modalities, pre-requisites are rock bottom. Anyone can walk in and do it and have a result, if they follow instructions.

When we leave the realm of entry-level holistic healing modalities and consider professional grade holistic healing modes, such as BodyTalk, acupuncture, naturopathy, and chiropractic--we face the need for considerable pre-requisites. Anatomy & physiology are two of these. So any way you learn Anatomy & physiology is a good way to do it. Why not practice on your self?

Without exposure to serious anatomy-physiology, students of professional-grade healing modes can feel overwhelmed by the number and complexity of physical systems.

In mainstream hospital doctor training; the stack of layered physical systems, genetics and drug interactions piled on top of your head is even worse and more boring than in most holistic modes.

Old-school hospital doctor training is more interested in operating equipment and drug interactions. This is appropriate for trauma medicine. In comprehensive holistic healing modes, we are more seldom faced with car accident victims and more interested in the emotional aspects and the invisible causative aspects of symptoms.

Wonderful as these are to perceiving the whole person, they the added topics can add to student overwhelm.

If there were already lots of books on simple ways to navigate invisible energy, I wouldn't have bothered writing this one.

The NEW Energy Anatomy attempts to bridge this gap, fill in this gap, and show, how doing so SIMPLIFIES both the learning and practice of holistic healing, across a wide

NEW Energy Anatomy

range of modalities.

Beyond body, image, front~back-, top~bottom, right~left virtually all our invisible-energetic systems and subsystems are primarily expressions of our etheric body and etheric formative forces. I think this paraphrases Steiner pretty well and I think it still has much merit. Properly understood, each system-subsystem in our psyche, PACME, lives, moves and has its being in the 'energy envelope' of our etheric body.

Q: Why not write a book on the anatomy of the etheric body?

A: It's been tried by the Theosophists. These books are neither practical nor useful once muscle testing is available to explore with.

Believe me, I've thought about an etheric text. However, too big a gap exists between the studies that would have to be brought together in one text. The intellectual effort to bridge the fruits of etheric studies between 1890-1955 and the fruits of holistic healing modes starting in 1970, would of interest to few people. Too intellectual. Better to muscle test, meridian trace and learn how our energy moves and how to manage it better.

NEW Energy Anatomy makes use of the following views to locate unresolved unconscious disturbances:

- Single cells, blood, glands, organs, muscles, tendons, bone, bone marrow.

- Laughter Yoga's four vertical divisions of frequency in the etheric body [[laughter body image]] Babinetics.com has the topic of how to use this for healing (laughter arranged by frequency corresponding to stable vertical sections of our body)

- Right~left, YANG~yin (the whole person expresses as a TEAM effort, rhythmically alternating between YANG active expressions and yin expressions of enjoyment and self-care)
- Front~back, Conception Vessel~Governing Vessel (the two stable "pillars" in our unconscious, self-esteem and self-concept)
- Top~bottom, conscious self (neck-up only) basic self (neck-down, immune system) More precise image: from the diaphragm muscle down (another perspective on the two main team members)
- The four etheric elements earth, air, water, fire. (if you can test for the priority element to treat, you are closer to finding the priority meridian. This is an aid to therapeutic direction)
- The seven classical etheric centers (least useful of this list, in my experience, because so manifold in meaning, expression, depth, interpretation).

In addition to these basic reference points, a partial list of Unconscious patterns exists very useful for checking when self-healers get stuck—which is often. If you are stuck on an issue, with a good list of Unconscious Patterns, you can test thru them like a set of lenses to see which one gives you a better view of the invisible causative agent you are tracking.

Our psyche is encompasses several RANGES of frequency. If you have no way to navigate, everything looks the same—and it is not.

This relates directly to the good-news~bad-news of navigating human energy exclusively by means of auras-chakras-meridians: everything has a tendency to flow together into everything else.

Physical anatomy has a relatively narrow range of frequencies. Different tissues look different. Human energy does not have this limits; it's ALL energy.

NEW Energy Anatomy

This means self-healers and energy practitioners must have two things within themselves:

* Coherent models of how energy is structured,
* A method for making experiments in navigating issues.

The challenge for self-healers and practitioners is to learn and navigate within an energetic landscape of frequencies, far wider than physical anatomy.

Muscle testing is hard to beat for navigating your way within the invisibles of the human psyche.

Apart from muscle testing, Goethean Holistic Science methods, which some of you will know are at the basis of Waldorf-methods educating, has practical suggestions for how to begin such studies. One of them is to *start with the most obvious discernable polarities*. Work toward details as time and interest permit.

The most obvious 'frequency structures,' or polarities in our psyche are, in no particular order:

- A range of frequency high to low from TOP to BOTTOM, crown of head to toe.

- A contrasting polarity, a rhythm of, YANG and *yin*, alternating between RIGHT side of our physical body and *left* side of our body, from the neck down. This contrasting rhythm is most active and visible in our digestive organs.

- Contrasting electrical and magnetic potentials, front and back in the body. Our conception vessel (CV) in the front of the body is our magnetic potential. Our Governing Vessel (GV) on the back of our body, is our electric potential.

HealingToolbox.org

Within these contrasting polarities or see-saws, are most the topics of this book.

Each pole is supposed to work with its partner as a teammate.

How well or poorly each pair of poles is collaborating is very easy to measure with muscle testing of any kind.

Short version of your own Energy Anatomy: Inner Dashboard

Readers who become familiar with both their lower and upper quadrant systems will enjoy the Inner Dashboard, a simple map of the eight quadrants.

For any energetic target you wish to explore in your psyche, mapping how your target is located in your eight quadrants will immediately tell you where the priority place is to address, your weakest link on this issue. The Law of Rumi encourages us to always work where we can remove blocks and obstacles to the qualities we wish more of.

Find full discussion here, "Inner Dashboard: Easy Energy Self-Assessment for self-healers"
http://healingtoolbox.org/k2-stub/item/400-inner-dashboard-easy-energy-self-assessment-for-self-healers?highlight=WyJpbm5lciIsImRhc2hib2FyZCIsImlubmVyIGRhc2hib2FyZCJd

How to navigate a range of frequency

waking <=> dreaming <=> sleeping

Later on we will see a RANGE of high to low frequency is often also a range of TIME, new to old.

9

NEW Energy Anatomy

This is a big idea and also correlates like this:

Waking	conscious	words
Dreaming	SUBconscious	feelings
Sleeping	UNconscious	needs

Find specific language techniques for downshifting from words into feelings and from feelings into needs in Compassion Communication (CNVC.org)

What was wrong with auras, chakras and meridians?

For those with a memory of the forty years of holistic health and healing, since 1970, it's pretty darn clear, auras, chakras and reflexology points; while common, are also commonly confusing to beginning students. Textbooks quickly become technical, narrow and specialized. Each indeed is a study unto itself, can occupy you for a lifetime.

Some of this mentalness is natural because the topic, human energy, is primarily invisible. Great focus is required to penetrate the invisible world and make it your own.

Adding to difficulties with auras and chakras, clairvoyant perception is required to have a direct experience of these.

That was before muscle testing.

Let's draw a 'line in the sand' and agree 1990 represents when Touch for Health converged with NLP, muscle testing began to be applied to more precise ideas about our unconscious. Since 1990, muscle testing has been applied very extensively to invisible human energy by energetic healers with immediate need and use for access to and navigation of unconscious material.

Muscle testing is so effective, it has reduced the need for direct clairvoyant perception. Both muscle testing and clairvoyance track back to our sixth, discernment center, our etheric center on the brow.

Energy Detectives no longer need to be clairvoyant to perceive energy differences directly. They can test their way thru to verifiable and repeatable distinctions with themselves and with patrons. They can navigate their way into and around invisible energies with self testing. Since 1990 people in several holistic modalities are learning to trust the presence and reality of energy thru their own testing.

Can people be misled? Absolutely. That's why self-protection and 'checking your work' is continually practical.

Why human energy anatomy?

All anatomy is locating things. As they say in real estate, three reasons exist why people buy a house: location, location, location.

Location is also valued in a doctor's office when physical pain is the target. The doctor asks you, "Can you point to where it hurts with one finger?" Just locating where a disturbance is, basic geography, is very powerful.

The less visible your target is, the more IN-visible your target is, the more useful location, location, location becomes. Virtually every disturbance in energy work is primarily invisible. Exactly WHERE "my problem with my mother is" is not as easy to find as we wish and assume.

Physical things we measure with rulers and gauges. You

NEW Energy Anatomy

know what to measure; you can see it. Energetic features, especially invisible ones, require direct clairvoyant perception or kinesiology testing. Energetic anatomy informs you what is present to be measured.

NLP offered a breakthrough, VAKOG, which is an abbreviation for our primary sensory channels, visual, auditory, kinesthetic, olfactory and gustatory (smell and taste). Our habit body represents our unresolved disturbances thru memories written in these sensory channels. Locating and testing for the presence of these sensory modes is a major tool for clearing invisible targets.

Identify all the primary causative factors

Most people who come to Medical and Health Intuitives do not have all the primary causative factors in view. This is mostly an educational deficit, not any lack of intelligence in clients. If they knew where to look and how to test to verify and validate, and have a few simple tools to work on themselves, they can do much. Both energetic and physical anatomy help you locate and identify all the primary causative factors relevant to your target

This book presupposes ANY disturbance you wish to acknowledge, address and moderate is located SOMEWHERE in 3D space around your spine. This means either inside your skin or outside your skin.

The topic of 'You are a column of Light' can be fund in other Healing Toolbox articles and classes. Your vertical column of Light is roughly where your bony spine is. The nine views here permit you to locate target issues more easily whether inside or outside your skin. The more unknown or obscure your target disturbance is, the more useful NEW Energy Anatomy is to find your way.

When a target disturbance you wish to address is

unknown or obscure, anatomy is at least a map to find your way.

Energetic anatomy is MUCH SIMPLER and MUCH EASIER than internal human physical anatomy, so fear not!

Q: Which should I start with in a session, physical or energetic anatomy?

A: Depends what you wish to address. The more tangible your concern is, like pain, infection, and inflammation, the more useful physical anatomy is.

Conversely the less tangible your target is the more useful energetic anatomy is. For instance, most mental-emotional disturbances are primarily INvisible and yield their location, character and quality to K-testing. Energetic anatomy views narrow your search with dramatic ease so you can get to the specific issue or tissues to address for healing.

The strongest aspect of energetic anatomy views is: orientation. The intertwining of the organs, nervous systems, meridians and personal issues reveals itself only with practice.

Energetic anatomy is a scaffolding for your own understanding. You supply the Aha! Practice and your intuitive knowing will improve. Persist and you will inevitably accumulate observations of many kinds, and weave yourself a beautiful, serviceable robe of wisdom about how things connect in the psyche and affect the body.

For impatient people, feel free to skip forward or backwards to what's relevant to you. Most discussion has been moved to the back of the book. This is a handbook after all.

NEW Energy Anatomy

Why can't it all be One?

For those of you tired of making distinctions and who wonder when we get to the Oneness; you're correct, the endgame is Oneness, not more and better distinctions, oneness in LOVING, not in mentality. Oneness in the mind only, "from the neck up" only is bogus, ersatz, virtual oneness only.

That understood, we have no choice but to employ distinctions until we can let them go and use Oneness as our technique. As a healer friend, Sherwood Duane, says, "You can't let go of anything until you have it." So we use distinctions to find our way back to Oneness—and then we drop them.

Someone said love without wisdom is anemic; love without wisdom is often merely sentimental. When Love makes use of healthy distinctions, love becomes wise.

The Law of Rumi

The poet Rumi says we cannot go at Love, abundance or success *directly*. Rather we go at positive qualities *indirectly* by working on our obstacles to Love, abundance and success.

We go at our blocks and obstacles directly by any process of personal-spiritual growth. What in your Healing Toolbox.

How do we clear our blocks that? Well, most of them are sub- and unconscious. So unless Grace shows up, you have to make more healthy and useful distinctions up to the point where you can—let go.

Any positive quality you wish more of can be further unblocked and strengthened. "You don't have to know how—you only have to ask," as Maryann Castellanos of HealthyEnergetics.net says.

> If you get stuck, give a call,
>
> Bruce Dickson
>
> Los Angeles 2011

The paradox of mapping a hologram

The human being is a living hologram. Don't feel too proud about this; ALL living things are living holograms. Yours is simply more complex; and, has an eternal immortal aspect most life forms do not. Find a full discussion of holograms in the forthcoming hologram booklet.

Effective self-healers have some basic maps of our hologram, the human body and psyche

To map a multi-dimensional hologram, you end up with diverse, overlapping maps

Each map is the hologram seen from a different frequency or node in the hologram; hence, the relevance of the poem of the "Blindmen and the Elephant" here: http://en.wikisource.org/wiki/The_poems_of_John_Godfrey_Saxe/The_Blind_Men_and_the_Elephant

Ideally, these maps overlap and augment each other, different views of the same animal, the human being. How that works for you, the maps you will use, can only be determined by you, thru practice.

Very-experienced self-healers have all become very familiar with one or more maps of their own hologram. Over time, practicing on themselves and with clients, they internalize these maps; at which point, it can look like

NEW Energy Anatomy

"magic" to an outsider, unfamiliar with what they are accessing internally.

It's just practice. If you start where you are, and keep practicing, you will improve. Wherever you are now, with whatever maps you have in hand, is a good place to start.

Very clairvoyant practitioners have the added advantage of direct perception, to some degree, of how energies invisible to animal eyes appear and show up "on the other side." When clairvoyant persons practice, they evolve to the ability to "find my way with inner radiance," as John-Roger says on a recorded meditation.

NEW Energy Anatomy sequences some of these maps for the purposes of beginning self-healers and those who wish more effective maps for use and/or training purposes. Each map describes a human potential or capacity. If you know of maps I've missed, please let me know.

Any good map invites users to view the lay of the land; in this case, a human potential. Maps engender insight into where we are now, tools for finding where we are; and, where we would like to go. Maps give added leverage to identify and locate unresolved disturbances we might wish to access. Sometimes a map makes "what to heal" suddenly very obvious.

Where did this stuff come from?

"There is a simpler, more accessible and elegant energy anatomy. Where is it? If it doesn't exist, I will work on this," I said to myself around 1995. Then in 1998, sitting in the pilot class of the PTS Masters Program in Spiritual Science, apart from the course material presented by facilitators, the new anatomy seemed very likely to be based on the old real estate cliché, "location, location, location." This was one of the very few ways to escape all the wordy abstractions.

Bertrand Babinet's quadrant innovations (1985-1995) had multiplied access to the subconscious far beyond the inner child and family systems of John Bradshaw in the 1980s. Inspiration ran thru me motivating me to make whatever leap was needed to create something more clear and useful for accessing more of the sub- and unconscious. This had been my own particular healing journey. Virtually all of this book was in view, in more chaotic form, by 2000.

I was also determined if I did do this work, and it was successful, I would leave a wide paper trail for anyone wishing to follow me, on their own healing journey. Hence, all the books and couple hundred articles on HealingToolbox.org.

1998-2000 I wrote up most of the new views here; about 100 pages worth, of them, and offered them to PTS. No one was interested. Many years and many purifications later, here they are again. If you see corrections or improvements, please feel free to comment.

With clients, between 2001 and now, a locational approach has been validated as a crucial tool. It looks more and more as if much better Tools That Heal exist now than the old seven chakras model.

When Touch for Health and NLP began to converge in the 1980s, I suspected a clearer, simpler, more elegant, more practical energy anatomy could be born, if we had a few more puzzle pieces. I already knew it would *not* be based on metaphysical, clairvoyant technical data from the Theosophists and other Eastern-influenced literature and I knew why. Touch for Health had set a new standard of clarity and independent thinking that would have to be part of it. Muscle testing was going to be the main method by which people learned, explored and moved energy. I knew it would have to have the frequency of

NEW Energy Anatomy

Soul & Above as the Doctorate in Spiritual Science class.

I knew it had to be compatible with the meridian info and lore of Traditional Chinese Medicine (TCM). I knew it would have to be compatible with the useful parts of 20th century humanistic psychology, such as Carl Rogers, Virginia Satir, Gestalt, TA and NLP. I had seen how the brief bloom of psychosomatic medicine, 1955-1965, had died; and then, resurrected in the holistic health of the 1970s. I was pretty sure a LOT more coherence was possible here. I was certain psychosomatic medicine could be more of a science for people wanting to learn from illness and view it as metaphor.

Turned out this intuition was accurate. In addition to Bertrand, three other authors were all thinking and writing along these lines at the same time:

- Michael Lincoln who is here
http://www.talkinghearts.net/

- William Whisenant who wrote *Psychological Kinesiology*, which became of *Meridian Metaphors, Psychology of the meridians and major organs*

- Christiane Beerlandt (Netherlands) *The Key to Self-Liberation: 1000 Diseases and their Psychological Origins, 8th ed*, (2001) http://www.christianebeerlandt.com

Another question was, what is energetic strength? How do we quantify it? How can we measure it? What can we do to increase it? In this, Maryann Castellanos of HealthyEnergetics.net was a mentor and co-pioneer.

These topics continued to expand and ferment for another ten years in my own self-healing and in work with clients. Along the way, the success of *Meridian Metaphors, Psychology of the meridians and major organs* encouraged me to continue breaking new ground.

Meridian Metaphors is useful for determining which meridian-organ is holding onto which emotions, the axis of dysfunction, between undercharge and overcharge and some simple ways to use the Light to move these things off your self.

How to make your aura brighter

The more Coherent, Integrated and Aligned (CIA) you are, the brighter your aura will be. Brightness in your aura comes from the same places as brightness in any individual cell, from smooth integration and absence of blocks in the range of frequency from the inner Divine all the way down and into the 3D outer physical.

So here's another goal requiring us to go at it indirectly, by removing your blocks to Coherence, Integration and Alignment. We strengthen our life energy, by removing blocks to how Spirit flows thru us, from the Divine within us, thru our personality, and out to connect with other people. In making our aura brighter, life has to move from the inside out.

It's possible to address and clear our inner obstacles by becoming aware of, locating and then subtracting our unresolved disturbances. In terms of habits, usually we are realigning old habits with habits of a higher frequency, more closely aligned with Love, Light and Angels. I recommend the frequency of Soul and Above. If you find a high frequency that works better for you, please use it.

This handbook-manual is most of the distinctions I have learned over 20 years of which distinctions are really useful for locating and tracking invisible disturbances back to their origins—where they can be cleared.

Have your own Tools That Heal? Wonderful! Need more? See HealingToolbox.org or MSIA.org.

NEW Energy Anatomy

Q: How energetic anatomy differs from physical anatomy

A: Physical anatomy is location and visible detail of physical-material structures exclusively.

Energetic anatomy is location and whatever detail is possible and permitted of primarily invisible energy structures; and, their interplay and affect on physical-material things.

Etheric energy "behind" and underlying our material body infuses it with vitality and makes flows of feeling possible. Indeed our etheric body makes a physical vehicle for the soul on the material plane possible.

Kinesiology testing, K-testing, makes all these views verifiable in the domain of the individual experimenter.

Q: Do I need to be clairvoyant to use this?

A: Not at all. If you are clairvoyant, these views make even more sense.

The distinctions here will help you slow down your subjective impressions, so you can learn the notes, follow the lyrics; and finally, learn to sing the song.

This book will also be useful for anyone wishing to awaken, organize and integrate their own subtle and clairvoyant sensitivities.

Q: Why New Energy Anatomy NOW?

A: Beyond its use in client sessions, a burgeoning population of young sensitives and clairvoyants is growing up in our children.

The traditional study seven chakras does little if anything to address the basic difficulty of sensitive persons: a thousand energy events going on, all at once, and possible to see, too much going on, too little structure to know what to focus on, which way to go. I call this a *lack of therapeutic direction*. Auras and chakras per se provide relatively little therapeutic direction; or perhaps better said, for only a very few persons, who already have direct perception of these; and, a system to understand their unique perceptions.

When a system is out of balance due to too much activity, too much fluidity, the need is for more structure to organize the abundance of impressions. This is the situation most young clairvoyants, sensitives and empaths are in, overflowing impressions and too few reference points for what is mine and what is not; and, which direction to go. I was there too.

In terms of baby steps and "it's a cinch by the inch," the seven etheric centers simply not the best starting place for learning how human energy is organized.

The NEW Energy Anatomy follows NLP's suggestion to "chunk down" things that feel overwhelming into smaller, bite-sized, digestible bits. It adds some systemizing and sequencing to create a lower "ramp of understanding" for human energy and how we are "wired."

Etheric centers (chakras) are indeed part of this wiring but so deep in the unconscious as to be relatively inaccessible. The meaning and significance of much chakra activity and phenomena is far too individual to make any but the grossest generalizations about; and, if you have read any article or book on chakras, you have already heard those.

Looking at the topic of energy anatomy as Waldorf-trained teacher skilled in sequencing topics for learners, the study of auras and chakras, more naturally comes

NEW Energy Anatomy

AFTER a basic Energy Anatomy as presented here. That's all.

Aura and chakra perceptions can be measured but we have to start people with baby steps of measuring human energy. As they gain self-sensitivity, self-trust and self-confidence—and work with the Light for safety—they can apply their powers of discernment to more nebulous aura and chakra percepts.

Every aspect of NEW Energy Anatomy can be measured. Any low measures can be raised if you clear the disturbance tying up needed energy.

Make your own system if you can improve on this one. Send in your comments for the next edition and I'll give you full credit including your website link for anything used.

If you get stuck, give me a call.

v\V/v

The human psyche as One Whole and first distinctions

To reboot energetic anatomy towards things people can directly experience, without much clairvoyance; and, towards things they can directly measure, it will assist to go all the way back to the beginning, to the first lesson in Grade One mathematics in Waldorf schools:

What is One Whole in human energy?

Our psyche is One Whole, every part connected to every other part; alter one part and you alter the quality, character and flavor of the entire Whole. This is wisdom of the hologram.

The first obvious distinction: range of frequency

Within the One Whole of each individual psyche, the first obvious distinction is up and down: frequency. We can travel up in frequency or down in frequency. We can go from neutral to depressed; from neutral to elation, up and down. Everyone can go up and down in frequency in their own psyche.

The second obvious distinction: north and south

If we take "up and down" off the vertical axis and put it on a horizontal axis, the next obvious distinction is the psyche is a "two-way street," a two-way continuum of frequency, stretching forwards thru:

sleeping > dreaming > waking

NEW Energy Anatomy

and relaxing back the other way thru:

waking > dreaming > sleeping

Some readers will know this comes from Rudolf Steiner's *Study of Man* (1919). Indeed the task of the present text is similar in many ways. *Study of Man* was a throw-forward to the purposes of Transactional Analysis, the three selves, and NLP; along with, the aim to integrate human Divinity in how we conceive of our psyche.

Let's agree there are no fourth states of consciousness we have left out; let's agree sleeping-dreaming-waking covers both extreme ends and every frequency in between, in the human psyche.

If we intend this, we have established a scope and range of the psyche. Your range will be somewhat unique from my range, so this range thing will like many things, be primarily valid in the domain of one person.

Range and "choice"

We have unequal capacity for "choice" across our range, waking to sleeping. We have more choice towards wakefulness. Everywhere else, towards sleeping, we have less choice, less awareness and weaker intention. At the opposite end of "choice," we have "habits."

"Choice" is always in a dynamic balance with "habits." We would not be human without either one.

We have unequal capacity for "habits" across virtually our entire psychic range. We have more habits, doing more things, towards sleep. Everywhere else, towards waking, we have fewer habits and more choice and intention is more significant. In this context, only in making conscious choices are we 100% awake.

The lower and slower in your range of frequency, the further away you are from conscious choice and the closer you are to your habit body.

When Guru X says, "Just change that old habit pattern; it's easy, you can do it, go ahead and change it now," It's possible they are awake deeply enuf in their own habit body that they have discernment and choice available deeply in their unconscious. Most of us tho are only awake in the top 5% or 10% of our psyche. For us, it will take longer to alter deep habits we wish to upgrade.
Guru X's advice will not be appropriate to us because you can only acknowledge, work with and redirect habits you become aware of.

\v\V/v/

NEW Energy Anatomy

You have three levels of creativity

What's down there in my unconscious?

Have an issue you're working on, trying to get at? A good locational question is always, *How deep* is that issue?

We have different issues at different depths in our psyche, just like in the movie, Inception, where three different "octaves" of memory are accessed, three levels deep.

A HUGE benefit of client-controlled self-testing, self-muscle-testing of any kind, is ability to discern for yourself the DEPTH OF ISSUE, what depth an issue is active on. Correctly identifying the depth of your issue is a major locational key.

In *NEW Energy Anatomy*, and Best Practices in Self-Healing System, the closer you can get to your target issue, the more info you have about its location in 3D space, the closer you are to a solution.

This is not rocket science; this is real estate: location, location, location.

Even if you have no idea how to solve it, the more precisely you can locate it in your body relative to your spine, the more likely you are to find the primary causative factors—and therefore--solutions.

Q: This sounds very common-sensical. Why is this new?

A: It's not a new idea; what's new is the more direct ACCESS to this thru self-testing. Access to issues and habits in our lower and slower sub- and unconscious has primarily only been possible since around 1990. There is in fact virtually nothing written about this possibility prior to 1990. NLP from the 1980s had yet to converge with Touch for health from the 1970s.

Q: If it's so common-sensical, why aren't more people using it?

A: They are. But it's so new we are still in the phase of small circles of healers. Beyond self-healers and practitioners, people with immediate need for such methods, the topic is esoteric; many language barriers have to be overcome.

People do not like to confront problems they have no tools for. Being caught unprepared is embarrassing! The more Tools That Heal in your Healing Toolbox, the more confidence and courage you have to face a wider variety of issues.

We have three levels of creativity and responsibility

Human creativity exists on three frequency levels:

Conscious ⇔ sub-conscious ⇔ unconscious.

Everyone has these creative levels. Adults skew towards the waking-conscious pole; infants and children prior to puberty, skew towards the subconscious middle. Everyone goes unconscious during sleep!

All of us are creative on all three of these frequencies simultaneously.

You can think of these as three distinct radio stations, each broadcasting different material, each with a different "slant." Our rational yak-yak mind is the highest "radio

NEW Energy Anatomy

station" in frequency. If the content being broadcast contains a lot of self-judgment and self-criticism, then it may not be the healthiest radio station.

Our two lower frequency radio stations also play 24/7 in our psyche or we would not and could not be fully human.

I've found it's possible to change the station on my radio and listen to different channels. How about you?

Conscious creativity characterized

Making choices and decisions are prime functions and characteristic of conscious creativity. The best imagery is how an artist, sculptor, singer or dancer thinks. An artist makes many "choices" and "decisions" about what color-clay-movement to add, which NOT to add, and which to subtract. That's you, the Artist of Your Life.

"I think therefore I am," is self-concept, crating my story of "who I am." We pour a great deal of our adult life into crating something we like here, to become a person we wish to be. "My goals define me" operates here. Find a full discussion of self-esteem vs. self-concept in *Meridian Metaphors* with examples.

Sub-conscious creativity

This is our happiness, our happy-for-no-reason three-year-old, the bubbling up from inside of joy and gratitude, the happiness of our contented child within.

This includes happy, satisfied and contented memories from our family of origin. Don't have any? It's never too late to have a happy childhood. If you need a lot of demolition and new construction here, this is what guided visualizations and Ideal Scenes are for; these are major Tools That Heal in this frequency.

Most of our sub-conscious creativity goes into habits

Richard Bandler emphasizes habits is how humans learn. For better and worse, we learn thru forming habits, thru repeating and behaviors until we learn them; and then, performing them sinks down into our habit body where our child within can play them back as appropriate and timely.

Any behavior you repeat--your basic self will learn, it will take it seriously--whether you wish this or not.

Consequently, we have habits on every level of our psyche:

- Physically
- Imaginally
- Emotionally
- Mentally
- Mythologically and unconsciously

THIS is where most of our SUB-conscious creativity goes.

Our habits on all levels, taken together, can be termed our 'habit body;' or if you prefer, your 'habit hologram.'

Your conscious involvement in allowing-promoting-creating repeating behaviors on any of these levels summarizes and encompasses our conscious creativity.

Unconscious creativity

To understand your UNconscious creativity, you have to stretch and call up everything you know that works for connecting with and communicating with a three year old.

Our UNconscious is much less articulate than even our immune system.

NEW Energy Anatomy

In one aspect our happy-for-no-reason cells represent our UNconsicous creativity. All cells are born healthy as you can read about in *Radical Cell-wellness—Especially for women!*

In another aspect, the green Incredible Hulk represents our UNconsicous creativity. Left to himself, the Hulk knows what he needs and how to take care of himself. He rarely gets the chance tho, does he? When Hulk is disturbed, Hulk can express inarticulate rage, liver-rage, striking out indiscriminately at everything and everyone.

Now shift this capacity to the positive; imagine a happy Hulk. The second Hulk movie has a quiet scene in the rain, in a cave, with Betty Banner and the Hulk alone, while it rains. The Hulk is tamed and calmed by authentic connection, kindness and intimacy. That's always the direction for happiness for Hulk—and our unconscious creativity.

In another aspect, traditional fairy tales represent our UNconsicous creativity. You can see the some of the leading thinking about fairy tales in the various effort to "put right" various fairy tales. This effort began with Norbert Glas's "Snow White Put Right" which is here:

http://books.google.com/books/about/Snow_White_Put_Right_The_True_Value_of_a.html?id=6cL-MgEACAAJ

Others of these are on HealingToolbox.org. If you can write more of them, I encourage this because they help us move and back and forth between the waking self and the unconscious. This is rare.

In another aspect, gentle upward spirals represent our UNconsicous creativity. Unconscious creativity flowing up thru the body in GENTLE upward spirals is happiness in our sub and unconscious.

Explosive upward-rising energy as sometimes allowed-promoted-created in tantra and kundalini literature--is not safe.

Our habit body dreams of having a healthy middle ground of FEELING where Earth energy flows upwards thru the body in gentle upward spirals.

We may remember this kind of balance, from before puberty, in the relaxed enthusiasm of boys and girls in the "Golden Age of Childhood," age 11, fifth grade, before puberty makes us crazy and/or goal-driven.

"Intending" or "aiming" at the frequency of Soul & Above appears to be part of allow-promoting-creating gentle upward spirals, as adults. I don't claim to understand this completely; I have not accomplished this fully myself. I am working on it.

We have issues on three levels of creativity

Because we have three levels of creativity, we have potential and capacity for three levels of unresolved issues.

Conscious issues

Conscious issues are things we know need attending to and "fixing." If you have a yak-yak, "monkey mind," this can include the nagging inner voice of the Inner Critic, if you can hear its words.

Conscious issues are low-hanging fruit, easy to get at, the present disturbances we know about. We get at them primarily thru To Do lists, goal-setting and changing our behavior and habits by consciously redirecting our self.

A subjective scale of 1-10 (Likert Scale, see Wikipedia) can be used by everyone to measure the strength of

NEW Energy Anatomy

weakness of habits, no kinesiology testing required. If you can self-test, your accuracy in measuring using a scale of 1-10 multiplies.

Sub-conscious issues

Sub-conscious issues are fruit higher on the tree of our psyche, somewhat out of reach. These take more work to get at.

How to get at them? Sometimes you need to practice more with Tools you have or learn how to use a new tool. Putting time in on Inner child work and learning Compassionate (nonviolent) Communication are good examples. You can get to unresolved subconscious issues as you learn to listen to and communicate with your inner child.

Sometimes you don't have any Tool that will work and your only choice is to build a ladder. If you don't have a ladder at hand, you can *build* a ladder. I've built a hundred ladders and most of them, not all of them, worked well. If you build an effective ladder, you can get to new issues. My ladders always work better when I invite God to be my Partner in the planning and construction. Let me know what works for you.

Unconscious issues

Unconscious issues are the most difficult fruits to get to, highest up on the tree, most out of reach. From the view of standing on the ground looking up, these fruits can be both out of sight and out of reach high up in the tree.

How do you reach them? You have to either learn how to fly, or find someone who has already learned how to fly to go take a look at them and report.

Clearing unconscious issues takes the most willingness to

heal; and then, almost always a coach or someone else who has gone there before you and has comfortable working at that level of their own unconscious.

The above characterizes our three levels of creativity. If you can suggest more clear ways to express this, I welcome your efforts.

Three levels as words-feeling-needs

In Compassionate Communication, (NVC) we learn better language to acknowledge and discuss feelings. Below feelings we have needs.

Take just one step back and the Energy Anatomy perspective is obvious:

Words	**Conscious**
Feelings	**Subconscious**
Needs	**Unconscious**

If words sometimes frustrate you, maybe you are already awake to your feelings. Getting words, feelings and needs to all match up is challenging for everyone I know.

For me, giving up the word level and going for the deeper truth of my feelings and un-met needs is worth the effort.

Using self-testing to navigate our issues

These three frequency levels give us wonderful purchase on where a habit we wish to address is located. We can get around in these frequency levels simply by asking-- testing for—what depth this or that issue is at: conscious, subconscious, unconscious.

NEW Energy Anatomy

Knowing how to approach different levels of the psyche will be familiar to parents of children of different ages. Each creative frequency, each creative expression has to be approached on its own terms, exactly analogous to how you would approach a child, depending on their developmental age.

Q: How do I know which level my issue is on?

A: Each frequency feels different. If you will practice, you will develop sensitivity. Consider these three "flavors" of issues:

a) My issue is something I'm conscious of: I know what's bothering me.

b) My issue is something I'm only dimly aware of ; I'm not sure what's bothering me: My issue is in my sub-conscious.

c) I have no idea what's bothering me. I'm in the dark on this one!: My issue is unconscious.

Waking, Dreaming and Sleeping

Rudolf Steiner pointed out, to the first Waldorf teachers in 1919, how none of us is awake 100% all day long in our so-called waking life.

In fact we travel back and forth on this continuum between two poles, waking at one end and sleeping at the other end, all day long.

Rudolf Steiner made "conscious-subconscious-unconscious" into something imaginative and artistic. He analogized them to:

> ***Waking <=> dreaming <=> sleeping***

Waking creativity ~ thinking, choosing, deciding, initiating action, writing a letter, paying a bill, choosing one action over another action.

Dreaming creativity ~ daydreaming, feelings in general, our day-dreaming and night dreaming are all creative capacities.

Sleeping (unconscious creativity) ~ breathing, digesting, assimilating, peristaltic action, eye blinking and other reflexes; ultimately: all cellular activity. *Someone* is building your body, growing your hair, digesting your food. Who is that? We also have hunches, guidance and intuition and we don't know where these come from either.

Waking-sleeping-dreaming (WDS) points to the whole range of frequencies in the human psyche all at once and this is how Steiner used this idea as well.

WDS is a two way street; SDW is the exact same street walked the other direction.

Pretty good definition of maturity

A pretty good definition of maturity is at hand here. The more mature an individual is, the more wakefulness they have in all three creative levels of their psyche.

Our three levels of creativity make it easier to understand why we might be "of two minds" sometimes. One frequency is going this way; another frequency is going that way...

Waking, dreaming, sleeping in cell physiology

3) surface

NEW Energy Anatomy

2) function, cell organs

1) core

Cells know how to be healthy. It's negativity we are holding on to that makes them unhealthy. Most people I see in my field are unknowingly holding on to negativity in their sub- and unconscious. This story applies to me when I have sessions with my mentor.

Rudolf Steiner suggested how our three levels of creativity play out in our physiology:

We are most awake and aware in our nervous system.

In our muscles we have dim awareness of feeling and movement.

In our bones our conscious awareness is most asleep.

RS also suggested how our three levels of creativity and responsibility correlate with the Kingdoms alongside us here on Earth:

In our Sleeping we are akin to the Mineral Kingdom

In our Dreaming we kin with the animals and plants

In our Waking we are kin with other humans

How deep is my issue? The iceberg metaphor

If you ask, "How deep is my issue?" then Sigmund Freud's iceberg metaphor of the psyche illustrates "depth of issue" clearly.

HealingToolbox.org

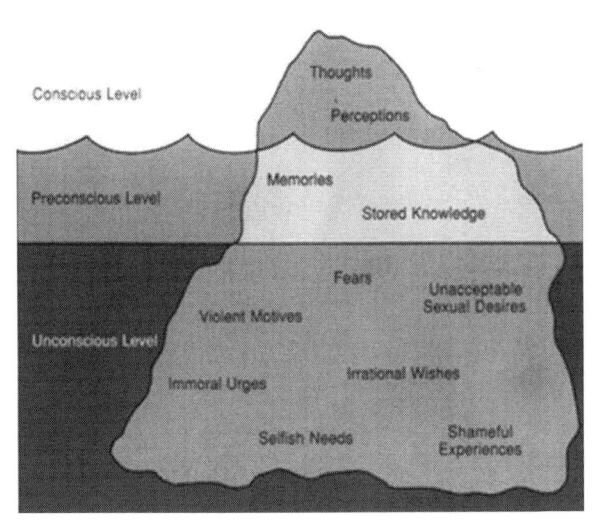

dg-iceberg Freud

Above the water line ~ The part we see above water, represents expressions, creativity, habits and behaviors we consciously choose and know.

Everyone has at least two more levels of expressions:

Just below the water line ~ Look over the edge of your boat, down into the water the iceberg floats in and you can see ice below the surface. You can see some ice there yet you see it only dimly; you see something-- but unclearly. This represents our subconscious.

In three selves terms, this is the basic self or inner child. Our subconscious attitudes towards life are held in our inner child. The waking self experiences these mainly as vague feelings of comfort or discomfort. Forgotten childhood memories from this

dg-iceberg 2

37

NEW Energy Anatomy

lifetime are also here.

You have at least one more deeper level of expression.

Far below the water line, underneath the floating iceberg is ice and ice shapes you cannot see at all from the surface. For example you cannot see the bottom of an iceberg from a boat on the surface. On a large iceberg, parts of your iceberg are so far underwater, light does not reach them; light from the surface is blocked by the iceberg itself. It's dark far under the iceberg.

Here we have memories, attitudes and mores invisible to the waking self. They include repressed childhood memories and orientations towards things acquired in prior existences.

Peeling the artichoke

The process of clearing our issues is analogous to peeling a cooked artichoke. Keep peeling; leaf by leaf, work your way towards the heart of he matter.

3) Top leaves ~ conscious issues, you know what needs to change here or any friend can tell you.

2) Middle leaves (subconscious issues) ~ you get to these thru communicating with the inner child. Anyone who can talk with your inner child can assist you to explore and redirect habits here.

1) Inner leaves ~ Core issues, unconscious. We are each blind and deaf tour own issues here. Sometimes we can still feel them. You have to ask for assistance to reach these. This is why we need each other to heal, a theme take further in Self-Healing 101! Awakening the Inner Healer.

Q: Your method is too technical for me. Can't I just

guess?

A: Yes you can always guess. Take a "shot in the dark," and see if you can locate your target by luck or dead reckoning. It may work. A subjective of 1-10 (Likert scale) is an under-used Tool That Heals; because, increased awareness alone itself is healing. The more comfortable you are using your Intuition, the more likely you can locate your target by dead reckoning.

For the many people who are kinesthetic dominant, who an navigate their inner life by where they feel "well" and "not well," they can *feel out* where their issue is without "looking for it" or "locating it," a visual strategy.

Language is leverage

Our unconscious memories, habits and behaviors are NOT hard-wired. However because factory-style K-12 educational systems except Waldorf ignore this dimension of the human being, few of us have much language for this material—and language is leverage.

It's dark down there! Issues can be hidden, cloaked and disguised here. You have to be an explorer or work with an explorer who's been there before to navigate in the unconscious.

Personal responsibility on three frequency levels

Because we have three levels of creativity and unresolved issues, we have personal responsibility on three frequency levels.

Conventional language tells us, "We are responsible for our creations on all levels" Three levels of creativity makes more clear what the heck they are talking about.

NEW Energy Anatomy

Q: Wait--I don't like this idea. My plate is already full. I don't need any more responsibility.

A: Then stop right here; read no further No urgency exists. Take your time. The only people who will enjoy reading further are persons looking to walk a path of greater self-mastery. This path is not for everyone all at the same time. It's primarily for those people who feel they cannot go forwards and cannot stay where they are presently. When forward is the only option available, the only direction available, then let's walk together because we very much need each other to heal. It's a cinch by the inch.

Our core issues often look like this: We can't fight our way out of a wet paper bag but people around us can see clearly where to push thru. This applies to me too.

Ask your worst enemy what's wrong with you

The above appears to be the wisdom in John-Roger's idea of "Ask your worst enemy." your enemy is very likely to see the chinks in your armor more clearly than you do. Why? Because we push our unresolved unconscious issues out and away from our body, as far as we can push them. We discard them and chose not to deal with them. Consequently they remain alive on the outskirts of our aura.

Out and away from our body, they are in closer proximity to other people than to our own waking awareness. Other people walking near us are walking thru our issues we have discarded. They may be feeling them more strongly than we ourselves do, especially if they are paying attention to us.

This ends a short introduction on the psyche as One Whole.

Our issues are like a game of pick-up-sticks

Remember the game of pick-up sticks?

dg-pick-up sticks

This game characterizes how our issues are in our habit body. How do you get to the red sticks that give you points and help you win the game? It requires time, intention, patience and gradualness, doesn't it? In pick-up sticks, you see the red stick worth 100 points on the bottom of the pile, beneath the rest of the sticks. But to go at it directly will disturb all the sticks above the red one. You forfeit points if you disturb other sticks above the red one. To get to the red stick you have to take off the top one, the next top one, the next and the next. Then the red one is revealed and lifts out easily.

There's a saying in self-healing, "peel the artichoke until you get to the heart of the matter." Our issues are layered. One session is not going to remove a core disturbance. A core issue is going to surface in layers.

NEW Energy Anatomy

Thank God for that. We couldn't handle it if the unresolved issues that caused our diabetes or arthritis surfaced all in one day. Instead Spirit gives us our healing in pieces, bite sized chunks we can handle. Usually there are many self-healing actions to be performed to go thru a core issue for the last time.

To switch metaphors, any chronic or serious physical illness is a diamond with many facets, a healing metaphor with many facets to it. Clear all the facets, you clear the condition. NLP by way of the Three Selves puts it this way, clear all the representations of your disturbance in your basic self and you clear the disturbance, by definition. Did we mention you do not have to explore every facet explicitly? Your intention to heal is the primary causative factor in your healing. The individual facets, the individual leaves of the artichoke, clear in related groups.

Core issues have many unconscious components to clear, by definition. Our unconscious issues often look like this: problems we can't solve that everyone else around them sees many solutions for. Going deeper is the only way to get unstuck for unconscious dysfunctions that keep hanging around. The language of the three selves helps people go deeper. That's why it's so popular with counselors and therapists, the first group to take hold of it.

Two great questions to begin all your sessions with

Asking two questions at the beginning of any session with therapeutic intent offer tremendous benefit to practitioners.

These two questions allow us to narrow the scope of inquiry into invisible realms; and, to measure the patient's therapeutic drive and momentum.

They respectfully permit fast-forwarding thru many pleasant but non-therapeutic yak-yak preliminaries both client and practitioner become trained into.

1) Check DEPTH OF ISSUE of the disturbance first.

2) Check WILLINGNESS TO HEAL in the inner child, your patron's silent partner, second.

Example of being of two minds

"Indecision" is classic language for how we become DISintegrated top to bottom. In classic indecision, on one hand I feel one way, on the other I feel the other way (just as strongly).

A friend of mine demonstrated this to me twice in ten minutes recently. She had both headache and stomach pains to prove how energetically and physically significant being of two minds can be.

This wonderful person, on one hand wanted to attend a business networking breakfast meeting. This is a meeting where professionals exchange referrals for clients. This included paying $350 membership fee plus $200 quarterly dues.

dg-two headed horse

On the other hand this person felt scared and apprehensive about spending the money while her income was low and she had yet to complete her elevator speech,

43

NEW Energy Anatomy

brochure and website, several things needed to be successful at such meetings.

At the same time this person was of two minds on a second topic. On one hand she had decided to withdraw from a long term friendship with another woman because, if I heard correctly, she felt the relationship was unbalanced; the friend was taking too much and giving too little.

On the other hand my friend appreciated the friendship very much and valued the warmth and caring that was still present, if not to the degree she wished.

When my friend talked to me she complained of headache and neck pain in the back under the occipital; also, upset stomach and occasional shooting pains in the stomach. The direction of her solutions seemed to be—as usual—to talk with the inner child and recognize she was tying to hold onto two contradictory directions, on two different issues, at the same time.

Ultimately, "You don't have to know; you only have to ask." Be open, use your senses, improvise and be spontaneous. You'll find your own way.

K-testers will be interested to hear that ten years of practice suggests client issues can easily be tested for their level of depth: is this issue at the conscious, sub-conscious or unconscious level?

.\v\V/v/.

Undercharged or overcharged?

If it's a disturbance, it's almost always either over- or undercharged. This is a good distinction to test for.

How does a violin string vibrate?

A violin string, a piano wire, vibrates both to the left and to the right of center, where it is at rest. In a similar way, in the body, we are as out of balance one direction in charge as we are in the other.

The classic sequence is this: We go down, undercharge, in one area. And then, compensate by going over in another area. That is the Conception Vessel, Governing Vessel "dance" in 25 words or less.

Maryann speculates that schizoid behavior is extreme expression of multiple under-doing, undercharge in the meridians. Reader comments on this basic research are invited.

Towards a theory of under and overcharge

Under and overcharge as energetic realities, in the meridians for instance, appears to be an established, mostly obscure topic, that up to now has been limited to the subculture of acupuncture.

Maryann and I got ahold of it from the Whisenant book, Psychological Kinesiology. A Google search now suggests no one else using under- and over charge as useful global questions to chunk down energetic disturbances into more manageable pieces. Let's change that now.

Despite the lack of literature, a theory of under and overcharge is surprisingly easy to articulate. At its simplest...

NEW Energy Anatomy

undercharge = empty; Overcharge = overflowing

It pays to remember, like everything else in Creation at this time, under and overcharge is primarily an EMOTIONAL reality:

Undercharge = empty = loneliness, nothing for me, low self-care, preoccupied with interior life

Overcharge = overflowing = unnecessarily reactive, possibly aggressive, all about me, preoccupied with outer life, possibly "too out there."

Under and overcharge are phenomena of the habit body, the basic self.

Undercharge = the b/s has too little energy, too little self-care, perceives itself as ineffective in the 3D world.

Overcharge = b/s expresses to much energy, is too full of self, possibly overactive, possibly has the habit of overcoming all obstacles by force, by over-doing

Metaphors for under- and over charge

Overcharge is everything Darth Vader. Overcharge is Rambo and violent killing video games. More artfully, overcharge is the Terminator. Cameron's Terminator robot, in all the movies, is an artful depiction of sacrificing any and all personal benefits for the sake of the goal. Terminator robots get beat up, shot, maimed and take no interest in their own welfare. That's right-sided overcharge. More generally overcharge is greed, ambition, and most of the seven deadly sins. The only undercharge sin is sloth. The rest are all over-exuberance of the basic self, the basic self connected with willfulness and willpower, which means the basic self is out of balance, out of willingness.

To sum up, overcharge is TOO MUCH OF SELF, over-exercise of the basic self tendencies.

A theory of undercharge

Undercharge is TOO LITTLE OF SELF, under-exercise of the natural and healthy basic self functions and tendencies.

My guess is undercharge usually follows overcharge; undercharge is the REACTION TO a prior overcharged condition. This would be the view from sequential embodiments. First you over-do it, then you under do it. First you try the perpetrator role, then the victim role follows.

A theory of balance

The seven deadly sins has a complimentary set of "contrary virtues" These are a pretty good expression of balanced expression between under and over charge. Note the mood of the following qualities when read as a group. Be sure to reference HEALTHY humility as opposed to unhealthy doormat, victim humility. The seven holy virtues are chastity, abstinence, temperance, diligence, patience, kindness, and humility.

A more complete discussion exists in the Meridian Metaphors, Psychology of the Meridians and Major Organs.

Defining some terms

Our conscious level of creativity is our yak-yak mind, the one we know so well inside!

This is our rational mind, either

NEW Energy Anatomy

      feeling dominant or

      thinking dominant.

Either can be dominant in an individual. Why both feeling and thinking can be rational was a topic spelled out in Meyers-Briggs Type Indicator (MBTI) in the 1980s and early 1990s and can be found online.

Waking creativity takes many forms, not just painting, sculpture and music. Because soul is choice, waking creativity can be a random act of kindness, writing a letter, paying a bill, spending quality time with your child.

See *You Have Three Selves*, vol. 1 for a full discussion of the distinctions between our subconscious and unconscious "minds." As shorthand here, we'll use RS's model of waking, dreaming, sleeping.

Dreaming creativity ~ dreams and day-dreams are often creative. Everyone dreams at night whether you pay attention to this or not.

Sleeping creativity ~ someone is building your body, growing your hair, digesting your food. Who is that? We also have hunches, guidance and intuition; and, we don't know where these come from either.

Check Willingness to Heal SECOND

Willingness to heal is the pre-requisite for all healing -- Bertrand Babinet (Babinetics.com)

The relevance of willingness to healing is demonstrated in health practices of every kind. Think about it; no healing takes place unless a willingness to heal is present.

One of the best discoveries to come out of 1:1 sessions with clients has been learning to check the client's willingness to heal--explicitly. Only as the inner child is at least somewhat willing and open, can disturbed parts and old habits be balanced. This topic is articulated for practitioners, coaches and healers in the booklet, "Willingness to heal is the pre-requisite for all healing " from Tools That Heal Press.

-=+=-

The above completes an elementary orientation to the human psyche as One Whole. Because these views of the whole psyche will be new to most readers, they can be unfamiliar. We make new things more familiar, by practicing them.

If you come up with a better way to explain ANYTHING in this book, do contact the author. I don't know everything. Like to help edit the next edition? That's open too!

-=+=-

The new views below apply universally to all of us. Each has clear, stable physical and psychological associations.

All topics below are measurable and accessible thru kinesiology testing protocols. Any testing method that works for you is fine with me. Full descriptions of measuring protocols and training is available. See the training course in **To Learn More**.

The Law of Gentleness for practitioners

A few words on using powerful Tools That Heal. At medical, nursing and chiropractic colleges, students are encouraged to "allow the body to heal itself."

In other words, understand that as practitioners it's

NEW Energy Anatomy

possible to make errors, make interventions that retard our client's healing process.

No practitioners is likely to make harmful interventions knowingly; but, what criteria are we supposed to use to determine if our intervention is aligned with how a body wants to heal?

Naturally the best way would be to ask the body directly.

Our immune system is primarily a subconscious Being, so it won't be speaking to us directly or sending us email or texts.

However with kinesiology testing of any kind, in the hands of an experienced practitioner, it's possible to "interview" the immune system, body and/or individual organs and systems to learn if this or that intervention helps or hinders it.

The above is easy to say now but is pretty new, only common in holistic healing circles since Touch for Health, then BodyTalk, then Theta Healing and so on.

Thousands of practitioners use muscle testing in varied methods and protocols every day now.

Even if you currently cant do testing of any kind, you can ask and guess. You'd be surprised how many healers and coaches don't need any muscle testing at all to test; they are already used to connecting deeply with people. They can simply ask—and know. So DO ask. If you are internally Coherent, Integrated and Aligned, the new CIA, you don't have to know what to do—you only have to ask.

If that doesn't work, check out *Self-Healing 101!*, PTS.org MSS program or some other way of learning to do self-testing, Client-Controlled Testing, that starts with self-sensitivity, feeling safe and that encourages you to employ an ecumenical God as you Partner.

The Law of Gentleness asks only one question

Simply ask: Is this body ready, for this intervention, at this time?

Your job as a practitioner is to discern a "true" or "not true" response from either the client; or if you have permission, to discern it by reading their internal response inside your own body.

That's it, the main question to ask.

It applies equally well to this herb, vitamin, intervention, technique, operation

Is it safe-beneficial-true for this body, at this time?

Q: Why does this work so well?

A: It works because our inner child, our 3D operating system, is the real expert on your physical body, not your rational mind. Your rational mind lives primarily in the heart and above, mostly from the neck up, relatively far away from the physical body.

If this question is *not* asked, the great downfall of effective practitioners is risked: doing too much, producing too much change, too quickly. That is, showing off. Practitioners and clients both buy into over-doing, doing too much, out of eagerness to 'make something happen.' Everyone likes dramatic, impressive "gosh, wow!" effects.

Yet whenever you raise the frequency of any portion of the body or psyche, the entire hologram of our health, body-mind-spirit, has to adjust up and may need time to detox, shed old materials no longer useful in your

NEW Energy Anatomy

hologram at its new frequency.

If you try to detox faster than cells in one part of your body are able to, and you create a healing crisis.

How to avoid a healing crisis

A physical healing crisis is more than you want to experience consciously. You can die or be permanently injured by a healing crisis. A story: My grandmother almost died after a very thoro and rigorous foot reflexology session. She was about age 65 at the time and had had no body work at all for decades. After this very strong foot work out she went to sleep, woke up around midnight and threw up EVERYTHING. She got back into bed very dehydrated. By the morning she was almost dead from dehydration and loss of electrolytes. She could barely phone a friend to come take her to hospital.

The healing crises I've gone thru as a client of other practitioners and my own self-care, have all been "interesting" but all in the vein of what NOT to do. Spiderman was right, "With great power goes great responsibility." The more access I have to sub- and unconscious levels, the earlier and oftener I check EVERYTHING with the Guidance, and Master Teacher of the person being treated, including with myself.

No one needs a healing crisis. I have yet to see any healing crisis that was karmicly necessary or useful. A healing crisis is a good example of an "unnecessary experience." All healing crises appears to be due to poor management by healers and coaches in charge.

First three etheric centers = your physical body

Readers and students of metaphysical literature are often

inundated-overwhelmed about the seven traditional etheric centers, a wisdom from ancient India. Obscured here is the bald fact that our physical body functions virtually altogether only from the lowest three etheric centers.

If you wish to grasp, understand and address physical body issues; then, physical health is 1 2 3.

The Law of Gentleness suggests asking the FIRST THREE ETHERIC CENTERS: Can this body handle this contemplated change, at this time? If any of these three lowest centers says "no" to any proposed change--and a practitioner goes ahead anyway--then a healing crisis is risked.

So I suggest, don't do anything in a session your first three etheric centers are uncomfortable with. This goes double for working with clients.

Q: How do I find out if the body can handle a certain intervention?

A: The only way to do this is by ASKING and TESTING. Kinesiology testing or any other intuitive testing is the way to go. If you do test intuitively, ASK each of the first three centers directly, "Can you handle this?"

v\V/v

NEW Energy Anatomy

NINE NEW VIEWS

~ View ONE ~

Right & left sides of the body, The magic of YANG & *Yin*

Without love, power alone is ruthless and reckless. Without power, love alone is anemic and sentimental ~ Unknown

> Those in love, want a partner. The real partnership is within the two sides, within ~ Maryann Castellanos
>
> Intuition is the *yin* of our psyche, inductive & deducting thinking is the YANG of our psyche ~ BD

Hidden in plain sight is the very striking contrast between the right and left sides of our body. Anatomically we are speaking first here of RIGHT~*left* differences from neck-down. Secondarily we will eventually talk about RIGHT~*left* differences from the breathing muscle (diaphragm) muscle down. RIGHT~*left* differences increase the lower we go in body image. If we start at the feet, the higher we go in body image the more converged the two are. This range of phenomena will become more clear later in this book after we discuss and expand upon Caroline Myss' hourglass metaphor for human energy.

It's common to hear people say, "I have more of my body problems on the right side of my body." Or, "I have more of my body problems on the left side of my body." If this applies to you as well, did you ever wonder why a majority of your health issues are on one side of your body? Ever wonder why other people have the majority of their health problem on the opposite side of their body?

Welcome to the magic of Right~Left (R&L) sides of the body, the easy place to begin a study of NEW Energy Anatomy.

Everyone reading this knows about YANG and *yin*. Introduced to Western mainstream culture in the 1970s thru popular translations of the *I Ching* and thru Macrobiotics, in 40 years, the symbolic language of YANG and *yin* has not penetrated as deeply as you might imagine.

A more experiential understanding of YANG~*yin* probably had to wait for more widespread self-muscle-testing.

Without personal experience with muscle testing or meridian tracing, people are mostly unaware of nor can they conceptualize YANG and *yin* well in their body.

Macrobiotics of the early 1970s was the first and last good literature on this in the West, supporting people to a personal direct experience of the contrast of YANG~*yin*.

In our post-2012 world, it appears the easy way to support people into a personal, direct experience of the contrast of YANG~*yin* is thru direct measuring of the relative strengths of each side of their body, from the neck-down and from the diaphragm down. Then awareness has something to work with to perceive these two expressions in our bodies and lives.

Human energy is organized right and left in our body.

The right side of our body, from the neck down, locates our capacity for YANG expressions.

NEW Energy Anatomy

The left side of our body, from the neck down, locates our capacity for *yin* expressions.

This is most strongly expressed in our digestive organs. Liver-gallbladder are much more active and creative. Stomach-pancreas-spleen are much more about savoring the goodness of life.

Dogs and cats as a fresh entry point to YANG~*yin*

If the difference between your two sets of digestive organs is too obscure, how about cats and dogs?

I ask you, "Which do you like better, dogs or cats?" If you like dogs better than cats, your personality preferences are likely to be more extraverted and your YANG side more well-developed.

If you like cats better than dogs—the opposite. Your personality preferences are more likely to be introverted and your yin left side more preferred and/or developed.

Q: Which is better, YANG or *yin*?

A: Whatever you have is best. This is not a contest. You want both sides working together as a team.

Q: What if I prefer cats and I'm right-handed?

A: This is not about dominance. The above applies to only your introvert (*yin*) and extravert (YANG) capacities, not to handedness; which is related, but not determinant.

Q: What if I like BOTH dogs and cats?

A: I do too. This suggests a good balance of extravert and introvert exists in your psyche. Look back on your life and see if there was ever a time when you did prefer either dogs or cats.

YANG & yin for modern minds, three views

Consider a sieve

Receiving is yin. A sieve is receptive but never contains.

Receiving is yin yet containing is YANG. You want both, right?

Dg- sieve

Consider a baby chick exiting its egg

Consider a baby chick with its cutting tooth, pecking its way out of its eggshell from the inside. Let's run that backwards and slow it down. The initial egg as passive, unbroken, restricting container, holding back the chick form 3D life, can be characterized as *yin*. The action of the chick, using a cutting instrument, is the YANG, breaking the impassive, limiting container, stepping thru restriction, pushing outside the limiting container.

Consider Grail and Sword

In classic symbology and Christian symbology, the Grail is the feminine container, the stillness, holding truth, inward-seeking. Also known as the Cup.

The sword is the action of action! Anything that breaks the mold of the old and creates a new mold, a new pattern, a patterns that works better.

NEW Energy Anatomy

This becomes Christian symbology as Lucifer was the old mold-format-pattern for souls to return to Oneness. The old patterns was "Law & Order," by the rules of karma, an eye for an eye and a tooth for a tooth. Christ is the sword making the new mold-format-pattern of love,-compassion-Grace-learning. The new way for souls to return to Oneness is thru demonstrating they are informed and educated to sins of murder, dishonesty, gluttony, etc.

The etheric body as yin container, the astral body as active YANG

This is approximately how the medical section of the Anthroposophic Society (Rudolf Steiner) talks about these two bodies. You can look up this technical distinction googling the words: astral etheric; and the phrase: "Anthroposophic medicine."

This is why our immune system devolves from and is more allied with our etheric body. It is the container, the maintainer, the preserver, the Vishnu force.

This is why our thinking self, is more aligned with our astral body and has a capacity for action often at odds with what's best for our own immune system.

Within this topic, I believe, is the key to sorting out immune disturbances and T1 and T2 immune disturbances.

Consider the yin-YANG symbol

The larger black and white swooshes are pretty easy to grasp. What's up with the smaller spots? Traditionally white is YANG. The spot of black in the white YANG of action is gentleness. The spot of white, in the black yin of inwardness and receptivity, is willingness to act in preservation; as in, a mother protecting her child.

Consider a mountain. On any mountain, there are always two sides. Chinese philosophers point to this as poetry for YANG and yin:

YANG is the sunny side of the mountain, yin is the shady side of the mountain.

dg-2 yin YANG

Consider: The right side of your body is naturally a bit more sunny and active. This will especially be true if you are right-handed.

The left side of your body is a bit more shady and relaxed—especially if you are right-handed.

On your right side, beneath the rational mind, in your subconscious, your liver is the organ capable of joyful shouting activity.On your left side, beneath the rational mind, in your subconscious, your stomach and pancreas are the organs most involved in peaceful savoring and gratitude for the tastes, pleasures and contentments of the day.

Traditional Chinese Medicine students will recognize these as TCM ideas.

NEW Energy Anatomy

So a key to why people have more health problems on one side of their body, right or left, than the other side, lies in these two characterizations and their natural contrasts.

Q: Why is this simple pattern and its manifold significance so little discussed?

A: My guess is perceiving R~L as a pattern in our psyche, as a pattern in the human experience, may require a foundation in the Three Selves; where, these contrasts are viewed as normal, complementary and as two members of the same team, working together, for the highest good of the entire system.

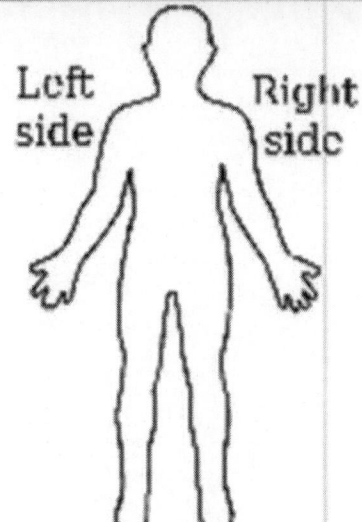

Dg-3 mountain sides

Conventional, mainstream 20th century psychology generated language geared almost exclusively about and for the unified, single viewpoint of George W. Bush's "decider," what Ernst Lehrs calls the objective, "isolated, one-eyed, color blind" viewpoint of our waking-conscious-rational self.

60

Right and Left in English and Spanish

How we are screwed up yang~yin in English shows in the phrase, "I like," when you compare it to the analogous expression in Spanish, "me gusta."

In English "I like" connotes an active process, an active outer process. "Me gusta" translates into English as, "It pleases me." This is the subjunctive case but more meaningfully, it's receiving, taking in, taking in nourishment. It's yin. "I like" is very yang by comparison. So in English our main language for expressing yin is very yang.

Right and Left as boy and girl numbers

In the early 1960s some elementary math teacher got a job as a writer for the math volume of a general interest home encyclopedia series for children. For a time, before the internet sets of home-use encyclopedias of various kinds, were sold in supermarkets.

This unknown math teacher shared wisdom he or she knew from Pythagoras as a way to bring the contrast of odd and even numbers alive for six year olds: odd numbers are boy numbers; even numbers are girl numbers.

Pythagoras' original idea was something like this: an odd number of points make more angular and irregular closed forms; starting with triangles. Even numbers of points make much more regular; and possibly more beautiful and balanced forms, starting with rectangles.

At schools, the contrast between groups of boys and groups of girls can be striking. This is very connected with why in high school and adult sports are separated by boys and girls.

NEW Energy Anatomy

Pythagoras' simple correlation is not popular today, discounted, ignored. Only four results exist in Google search. My Waldorf teacher training opened my eyes to the usefulness of discarded ideas, for the purpose of educating young children; hence, my original interest in this.

I now view the contrasts between "odd numbers" and "even numbers" as a wonderful reference for adults to perceive distinctions between their own right and left sides of their body and digestive organs, right and left.

Right and Left as digestion and assimilation

Another good way to perceive energy differences between R~L is the overlapping yet contrasting functions of digestion and assimilation.

Our right-sided culture is more aligned with digestion because it's closer to eating and when we eat, we often feel our stomach and duodenum.

I imagine many people equate eating with digestion; and erroneously equate digesting with assimilating. I bet many people assume eat-digesting-assimilating is all "doing," all active.

Given this confusion, the character of assimilation on our left is much more difficult to perceive.

The character of assimilation on our left is enjoyment. Savoring.

Q: Which organ is most aligned with savoring and enjoyment?

A: Our pancreas. See the four videos on psychology of diabetes at YouTube by Bruce Dickson.

Guess which disease, rampant now in the USA, is connected to this? Diabetes.

When we "can't get no satisfaction" as Mick Jagger of the Rolling Stones used to sing, this is our left-sided, *yin* capacity, out of balance.

The natural way to view assimilation, is collaboration between our stomach, pancreas, spleen, small and large intestine. They are our 'taking-in organs,' the assimilators.

Where are liver and gall bladder? They are busy making chemical components, non-essential amino acids, bile for fats; and, enzymes the pancreas does not make. Albumin, the major plasma protein, is synthesized almost exclusively by the liver.

Our right-sided organs of digestion are "makers."

Our left-sided organs of assimilation are "enjoyers."

So which are you more like in our life?

Are you more a "maker," always doing, doing, doing?

Or are you more an "enjoyer" letting waves of pleasure wash over you as you lie on the warm beach.

Or do you wish a BALANCE of these two?

Probably you want a balance of these two.

To find out how in-balance you are, simply measure each side, from the neck down separately

NEW Energy Anatomy

Our two nervous systems play out R~L

Staying with physiology, the largest energetic difference between right and left sides is embodied in our nervous systems.

According to MBTI, about 60% of us in the West prefer using our cerebral nervous system over our enteric nervous system.

About 40% of us prefer using our enteric nervous system, out gut brain, more than our cerebral nervous system for making decisions.

Briefly the cerebral brain corresponds to our left brain; our cerebral nervous system expresses thru the right side of our body.

Our enteric brain, in brief, corresponds with our right brain; our enteric nervous system expressing thru the left side of our body.

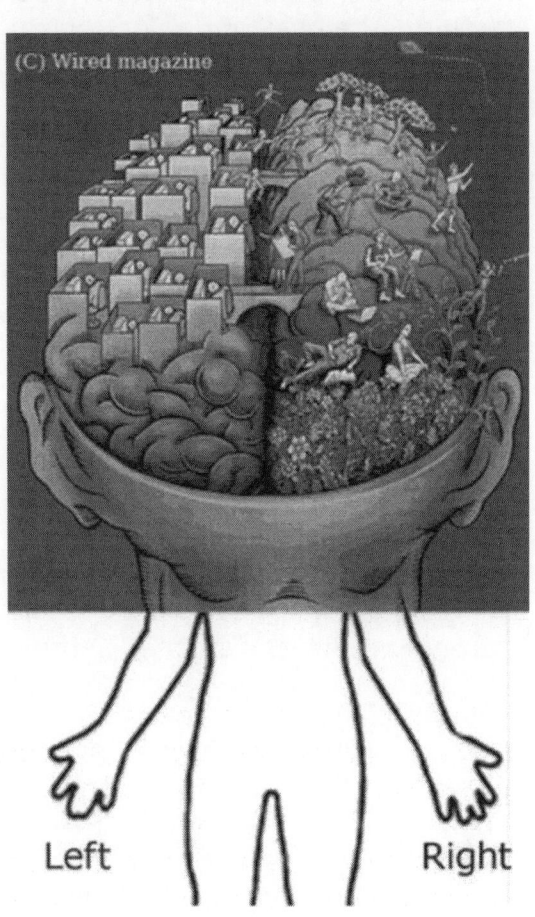

Dg-4 wired brain hemispheres

Which is better? Both. Integration is better; cooperation and collaboration is best, always.

Readers of this author's other books will recognize the theme of "two brains" here: two equal quantities of nerve tissue, two places of awareness in the body, but only one is dominant. The other is the supporter. Just like we have two hands, one hand is dominant AND life is easier with two hands than with only one.

For a full discussion of our two brains, see *You Have Three Selves, The clearest map-model of the whole person*, vol. 1.

Your rational mind can be either thinking or feeling

Adding to individual variation, your rational mind can be either thinking OR feeling dominant; either you prefer making decisions from your gut; or, you prefer making decisions based on logic.

Q: Which is better?

A: BOTH. Integration is better; cooperation and collaboration is best, always.

Q: What dominance do MOST of us have here in the West?

A: Because we attend so many years of intellectual-focused schooling, most of us are cerebral dominant. We prefer making decision thru thinking and logic.

All the following views of right and left sides (R~L) will help you see in your own body which side is dominant; and, if your dominant side is under- or overcharged. These are the keys to understanding why you have more physical concerns on one side of your body, if that is the case for you.

NEW Energy Anatomy

All of these "views" can be measured but these are the easiest to see without any measuring required.

R~L as "love" (active) and "be loved" (receptive)

When men and women are "looking for love in all the wrong places," they are usually looking for the experience of "being loved."

This is the natural-normal-healthy experience of love on the left side of our body, the kidney yin version of love.

If our capacity for love is intact on our RIGHT side we say, "I CAN love," we're comfortable with the actions of demonstrating connection and commitment to another, to others.

If our capacity for love is intact on our LEFT side we say, in English, "I am lovable." We can also say, 'I am lovable just the way I am now." Note: NO doing on the left; it's BEING.

Our mainstream culture and electronic culture is al skewed heavily towards the right side, towards *love as active verb*, towards *love as doing.*

This is all fine but when we expect YANG strategy and tactics to results in the experience of RECEIVING love then we are indeed "looking for love in all the wrong places" and will be disappointed.

Years ago in an interview with Tommy Lee Jones, he was asked what's your approach as an actor? He said, "To arrange things so the director gets to see what he wants to see." On our left side, in kidney yin, we are always and forever attempting to *arrange things to get our needs fulfilled.*

That's all the left side can do. That's part of the nature of the left side, to want, to need, to long for, to hope. Sound familiar now?

When we experience love on our left side do we jump for joy and shout to the rooftops? No, that's the right side. On the left we feel GRATEFUL.

This is why the image of the Holy Grail was so meaningful in medieval times. It was an artistic symbol for the experience of looking up and being filled from above by the water, the wine, of healthy loving.

The modern image is much more cognitive, the idea of into-me-see: loving your self, inviting others to come in to your field and share the love with you. If you are lucky, they do the same for you.

R~L as masculine and feminine approaches

The sword is a classic archetype for all things YANG.

The cup; yes, even The Grail, is a classic image for things yin. If the idea of a feminine and a masculine approach to life is uncomfortably sexist to you, think of this contrast as kidney yin and kidney YANG as TCM suggests.

A masculine approach to life (kidney YANG) is to ask directly for what you want, reach out for what you DO want, say yes to what you want. Reach for the brass ring on the carousel ride.

A feminine approach to life (kidney yin) is to ask INdirectly for what you want, to say NO to what is NOT wanted, to turn away, push away, when displeased. On the left side, we remove our self from what displeases us.

The MALE approach becomes dysfunctional in jumping the gun, behaving too aggressively, and being a bull in a china shop, often, on the emotional level.

NEW Energy Anatomy

The FEMALE approach becomes dysfunctional in behaviors of whining, complaining, gossip and manipulating. If a person cannot back up their wishes with actions, decisions and choices for meeting their emotional needs, resentment is a common result when they don't get what they want.

R~L as fight and flight

If we dial up the characteristic reaction of human energy on our right side, we come to FIGHT. If we dial up the characteristic reaction of human energy on our LEFT side, we come to FLIGHT. Fight & flight are neutral; we can choose to use one or the other for positive purpose or a negative purpose; in themselves, they are neutral.

What we are mainly interested in energy healing, is UNNECESSARY expressions of fight & flight.

Unnecessary fight looks like anger; unnecessary flight looks like retreat, withdrawal, hopelessness and giving up.

Our fight & fight response to life and people are HABITS; they are firmware; you can change them and moderate disturbed habits of fight or flight if you set your mind to it.

Seeing YANG and yin in your own body:

R~L: Bogart & Bergman in "Casablanca"

The contrasting characters of R~L sides, here in the U.S. was captured wonderfully by Humphrey Bogart and Ingmar Bergman in the movie, Casablanca (1942).

Rick, is our right side, who as the script begins, is

somewhat immobilized in his capacity for action. By the end of the film he has "done the right thing" and is again in alignment with his values and ethics.

Ilsa, is our left side, who is preoccupied with her needs for safety, for material security and getting her emotional needs met.

Just about anything you, the reader, know about these two characters in the movie Casablanca is useful for finding your own right and left sided capacities.

Are you starting to get an idea of why you have more physical problems on one side of your body? Which kinds of behavior do you have more stress with, Rick's or Ilsa's?

Q: Is the American national character still as polarized as Rick and Ilsa are portrayed?

A: No, 70 years later we are much less polarized but the way we think about male and female, right and left sides and the roles associated, has changed not as much as you might like to think!

R~L: Harold Hill & Marion the Librarian in The Music Man

Harold Hill is the brash, talented salesman who is also a deceptive huckster. Everything about him is extraverted. Marion wears glasses, reads books, sees thru the local phonies and is inarticulate about her objections, all according to her stereotype. She bares her beautiful soul only in song; he can barely sing at all.

The YANG-yin contrast between Professor Harold Hill and Marion the Librarian makes even more sense as a classic MBTI contrast between ESTJ, the classic American male archetype of the 1930s-1940s and INFJ the idealized

NEW Energy Anatomy

women-feminine counterpart of the 1930s.

Our right side is our Arnold Schwarzenegger side

Our liver, gall bladder, right kidney and some other internal structures on our right side, taken as a group, is our inner Arnold Schwarzenegger. This holds true for both male and female bodies, whichever you have currently.

Arnold Schwarzenegger's biography is very public. It's obvious he has both physical vitality and an energetic personality. It's easy to see a similar quantity of strength in both Arnold's physical body, in his body building, and in his "personality body" in his role as Governor. It takes a lot of vitality to run for Governor and put on a "show" as leader of California.

Our right side is our "Go for it!" side where we reach out into the world to strive towards outer goals, grab what we can grab, do what we can do, and get what we can get.

Our right side has to do with goal in the outer world. To accomplish them we reach out towards them, to handle them, to manipulate things to get the results we wish in the outer world. We go out and do the best we can, out in the world, to achieve our outer goals.

Our right side, as ads for the Armed Services like re mind us is the side of "be the best you can be," "A few good men," The Brave, the proud, the true," all right side, YANG, capacities. Go ahead, stand up RIGHT NOW, strike your best body builder pose and feel how it feels!

Readers familiar with MBTI will understand how our right sided YANG capacities align with Extraverted Sensing (ES) : hunting, tracking, sports, combat, competition, etc.

Readers familiar with the Inner Court model , the close-up of the habit body, will understand how Lancelot and

HealingToolbox.org

King Arthur characterize our left brain and our right side.

Ingrid Bergman & Judy Garland are our left side

Our left sided organs, omentum, stomach, pancreas, spleen, in that order of wakefulness, have a very different quality. On our left side we reach out to receive, to be touched, we reach out for what we need emotionally, to arrange things to get our needs met.

"Needs" here means physical needs: nutritional needs, intimacy and sexual needs; or, if you prefer a shotgun: "emotional needs."

MBTI students will grasp iNtuitive Feeling (NF) especially characterizes our left-sided expressions and behaviors.

Inner Court students will recall Guinever and Merlin (the inner grandparent) characterize the left side of our gut brain.

"Four hugs a day" is for Guinever and Merlin, not for our inner Arnold.

Dg-8 guin-judy-ingrid

The left side is indeed our receptivity, our "smiling energy."

NEW Energy Anatomy

Isn't this just Kidney YANG, kidney yin?

Q: Aren't you repeating what is already known in Traditional Chinese Medicine (TCM) acupuncture: kidney yin (earth) on the left and kidney YANG (warmth) on the right?

A: While kidney yin (left) and kidney YANG (right) is a crucial aspect, right and left sides encompasses many more topics including all those below not articulated anywhere else I know of. If you find other or even better literature, please let me know!

RIGHT sided YANG expressions

Liver, engaging with the world and its people and elements

Assertiveness in the outer world

Reaching out to give what we can give and take what we can take

LEFT sided yin expressions

Smiling energy is in some Chi Gung practices

Omentum, stomach, pancreas, spleen

Arranging things to meet our own physical and emotional needs. Later will we expand this to include spiritual needs, the need for connecting with our own Divinity, in our own, unique way.

Receptivity in inner and outer worlds

Reaching out to take in what we need and take in what is

offered.

Healthy Yin as "the still small voice within"

In listening more and more to my own "still small voice within," I realize, in a general way, it comes from the yin part of my psyche. I don't perceive it as decidedly left-sided; however, because my still small voice is 100% of the time pointing to opportunities to make choices better aligned with my own personal self-care, comfort, safety and convenience and that's all left side.

Healthy Yin is not "passive" and not "surrender"

Viewed by Western, hyper-YANG, macho males, "surrender" equals weakness. In macho-speak, we polarize the words "passive" and "surrender," coloring them to mean something negative, weak and bad.

Don't fall for this cultural domination propaganda. It's only over-charged male prejudice against yin in general and undercharged yin specifically.

Q: How do we reframe "surrender" and "passive" so we n longer see them as negative.

A: By recalling how ANY capacity can be a two-edged sword, cutting equally well for the good or for ill, depending on the hand that wields it.

In this case, the negative connotations of both "passive" and "surrender" have become over-broad and not useful as awareness of our Divine Feminine, on our left side, is long-overdue for re-awakening.

The positive expressions of both "passive" and "surrender" are emphasized in counseling, growth and Cultural Creative circles. For our purposes here, only the

NEW Energy Anatomy

positive connotations of "passive" and "surrender" apply.

YANG~yin as healthy push~pull

Our right side is our "push" side. Our left side is our "pull" side.

On our right side, our liver-gall bladder side of digestion, warmth, strength and relaxed resilience. Happy, healthy well-adjusted, home-schooled and Waldorf teenagers often embody these traits. Healthy YANG is facing life with confidence and absence of anxiety, without againstness, ready, willing and able to create; and, take responsibility for your own creations, to the best of your ability. This is what we love about healthy teens.

Dg-9 two-headed-horse

Healthy YIN, on our left side, the stomach, pancreas, spleen side of digestion, is taking in nourishment, listening to the environment, TASTING the environment, repairing-restoring internal vitality (the spleen repairs blood cells if they have only minor damage), arranging things internally and externally to get your own social, emotional and sexual needs fulfilled. When the taste of life (pancreas) is sweet to savor, a person can sing for no reason!

Please note we can push and pull healthy a well as unhealthy things towards and away from us.

Dysfunctional pushing on the right:

Pushing towards healthy or unhealthy goals. Mmmm, chocolate cake!

Pushing people aside, pushing them down, stepping on their face so we can take up their space! We can be in denial and resistance about our own death. We can push away (deny the existence of, the facts about) global warming or the death of hyper-consumer culture.

Dysfunctional pulling on the left:

We can pull inside our own shell, shut down, turn off, retreat into fantasy novels, romance novels, telly novellas, or video games.

We can pull in people and manipulate them.

We can pull in, withhold and then deceive.

We can pull abusers and perpetrators into our life. We might do this so we can play a familiar victim role. We can enable dysfunctional perpetrators.

By the way, each of these functions and dysfunctions can be measured, quantified thru inner testing or kinesiology testing, K-testing, of any kind. A scale of 1-10, ten being optimal is handy. For dysfunctional qualities, zero is optimal. If you get stuck

Dg-10 Punch & Judy puppets

75

NEW Energy Anatomy

give me a call at Skype SelfHealingCoach or phone number at HealingCoach.org.

Related to this topic is the wonderful idea and experience of our physical heart as a magnet. Our heart center—not heart muscle--is on the Conception Vessel. A magnet can pull to itself what we attune to.

The archetypal power of the original Italian Renaissance Punch & Judy puppet shows can be seen at the very start of one of Franco Zeffirelli's movies; I think it's at the beginning of his "Romeo and Juliet," where a historically accurate Punch & Judy puppet show is briefly displayed.

Punch & Judy as topdog~underdog

Modern language for this topic comes primarily from Gestalt Therapy, "top dog & underdog;" that is, perpetrator and victim roles we play. This in turn tracks back to the Karpman Drama Triangle where the dynamics of victim, perpetrator and rescuer are discussed and diagrammed.

A "Punch & Judy show" is another therapeutic metaphor, a therapeutic mirror, for unresolved, invisible inner conflicts. Gestalt Therapy points out how top dog-underdog conflicts are vertical conflicts, top against bottom. In Healing Toolbox language, such conflicts are illustrated as between the top and bottom of the human hourglass, the conscious self above, the basic self below.

Punch & Judy puppets as "liver attacking pancreas-spleen" in TCM

When "push" and "pull" are at odds, push and pull become "liver attacking pancreas and/or spleen" in Chinese medicine.

Internal conflicts exist not only top and bottom in human energy but also right and left. A vertical conflict, top and bottom, is almost always accompanied by a corresponding horizontal conflict, right and left. Punch, is our hot-headed YANG right side (Lancelot-liver-gall bladder) and is prone to beat up our cool-quiet YIN left side (Guinever-Merlin pancreas-spleen).

Punch & Judy puppets as modern negative self-talk

Readers will be familiar with modern ideas of negative self-talk: "I know I'm a good person; but, I can't be successful (without-unless-until) (I feel better, have more money, have a supportive partner, fix my teeth) insert other deficiency need here... then I'll be happy." That's the classic refrain of our left side in pain; it perceives she cannot get her own needs met.

Because inner conflicts can be vertical or horizontal or both, we might take a step back and look again to see if our YANG and yin forces are in balance. When young, souls take sides and declares YANG is better than yin or yin is better than YANG.

R~L sides and altered states

Our left side is our ability to accept and states of being altered from our mundane rational mind, and in the West, our predominant right side. In the West our left side is our aptitude and appetite for experiencing altered states. This is the only way we have of saying this in English I know of so far. Comments welcome.

From another point of view, our right side and rational mind is an altered state—compared to the dreamy state of a child age seven or younger. Our right side is the altered state of limited, sharp-edged, 3D, materialistic

NEW Energy Anatomy

alertness. Our left side is then 'all other states.'

Consequently our left side has aptitude and appetite for swimming into, around and enjoying altered states that are dream-like, fuzzy and out of focus, compared to the "light of day" clarity of the cerebral nervous system consciousness.

The above suggests a big key for understanding drug addiction, especially in teens. If your family-school-culture continually denies your left-sided capacity to experience altered states; forces you to experience only the "light of day" of the rational, cerebral mind, you could get pretty tired of this. Especially so if your left side is well-developed; including, aptitude and appetite for other states of being. If this is high; then, you are likely to experiment with drugs and alcohol to get something going on your left side, to get some relief from one-sided experience of only the rational mind and its creativity.

Drug-induced altered states have a very poor record of success in the industrial West. Meditation and K-testing are the preferred doorways into altered states since the Renaissance. Drug-induced altered states remain much more appropriate for indigenous peoples without access to modern education. In the West our conscious self is already so strengthened, we have to be careful not to damage it with drugs.

It won't surprise students of the Inner Court to hear Guinever & Merlin, on our left side, are our capacity to experience altered states.

Our body is most polarized lower

Our YANG and *yin* capacities become less holistic and homogenized as we down the body from head to foot. Breathing muscle up, we're pretty homogenized. Below our diaphragm, our digestive organ are split into a very definite YANG team, liver-gall bladder and a very definite *yin* team, stomach-pancreas-spleen. Finally our YANG and *yin* are split into two legs that walk alternating, as a team.

In New View TWO, Caroline Myss will explain more about this in her hourglass image.

Our weak left-sided personal boundaries

The left side especially becomes dysfunctional about personal boundaries. The U.S. is a right-side-dominant culture. Consumer culture is all about saying yes to what you do want. Seldom are we asked to say no to what we don't want. Seldom do we exercise our "No" to what we don't want even in the areas of pollution, waste, radioactivity and EMFs. Since boundaries and personal boundaries are primarily about saying "no to what we do not want," all of us in the U.S. especially women, need encouragement to voice a healthy "no."

R~L as two halves of "self-confidence"

Right side:

- confidence to face life

- feeling clear on what I want in the outer world

- feeling worthy to share my talents and abilities in the outer world and get paid for my service

Left side:

- confidence you can arrange things to get my own emotional, nutritional and physical needs met

- feeling clear about how I support others (healthy

NEW Energy Anatomy

boundaries)

- feeling clear on how others support me

- receptivity to feelings and appreciations from the outer world and other people

- receptivity to feelings, intuitions and gratitude from the inner worlds and other Beings

- feeling clear about my roles in my primary relationship, in my family, and in my community

Notice how both right and left side expression have to do with meeting our own needs. God provides us with two "hands" so we can get our needs met here in this 3D world.

R~L as goals-projects~needs

An acquaintance of mine was working with a client in a demo. He asked, "What do you want?" he pointed to the common difficulty people have expressing a clear positive **dg-10 goals-needs** intention. It's clearly easier for some

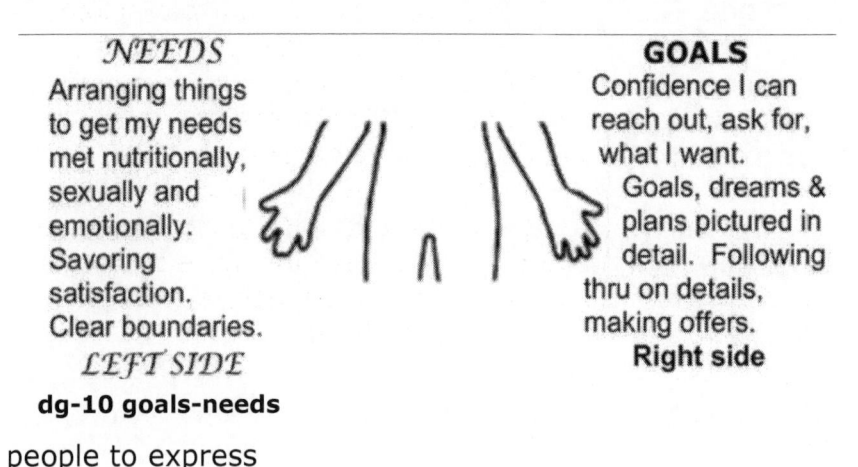

NEEDS	**GOALS**
Arranging things to get my needs met nutritionally, sexually and emotionally. Savoring satisfaction. Clear boundaries. *LEFT SIDE*	Confidence I can reach out, ask for, what I want. Goals, dreams & plans pictured in detail. Following thru on details, making offers. **Right side**

dg-10 goals-needs

people to express

what they do NOT want. This can be the away-from pattern noticed in NLP; it can also be willingness to complain.

In goal setting complaining can be used constructively, "Tell me what you don't want" can be the prelude to, "Tell me what you DO want." If the client says, "I don't want to be sick," you look for the opposite: I want greater wellness. He says you can catch people stating negative intentions in many forms. For example in, "I want to be more understanding and patient with my mother," "more"

dg-10 goals-needs

is a flag they wish to move away from some behavior or outcome they dislike.

The words "always" and "never" can also be flags that the person is trying to avoid a glass half-empty. Help them go towards a full glass so they can give from their overflow.

R~L sides as father & mother issues

20th century body-based psychotherapy in the 1970s discovered the pattern how issues with your father tend to be held on the right side of your body. Issues with your mother tend to be held on the left side of your body. This is a notoriously common factor in shoulder pain and tension. We'll revisit this useful generalization further below in the view of enteric and cerebral nervous systems. Giving credit where credit is due, my mentor on the topic of enteric and cerebral nervous system; and many other topics, is Maryann Castellanos, a Medical Intuitive in Encinitas, CA. Find her at HealthyEnergetics.net.

NEW Energy Anatomy

Right~Left as inner father and inner mother

The common pattern visible in people in the educated, electronic-ized West is people with strong inner fathers on their right side, from the neck down but great variability about an inner mother on the left side.

The inner mother of an individual can vary from a healthy balance with the inner father all the way down to less than 1/10 of 1% of an inner mother on the left side.

The lack of an inner mother is so common and widespread, one of the most famous children's books of the last 25 years is called, Are You My Mother? about a baby bird looking "in all the wrong places" for its real [inner] mother.

Our deficit of 'inner mother,' on our left side, from the neck down, arises from two main sources.

One is how we do--and try to do--everything out of our inner father, our YANG capacity. When grossly out of balance with the left side this is called "yang-banging" in Messages from the Body.

The other source of our lack of 'inner mother' is projecting, disowning and giving away our inner mother to external figures, images and fantasies.

This is "projection" in exactly the way it was used in 20th century psychotherapy. In 2013 "projection" can be conceived as "turned inside out." In this case perceiving our source of 'inner mothering,' 'self-nurturing,' as wholly and completely outside our own skin.

When we believe inner-nurturing is outside of us, our unconscious looks for a "screen" to project our disowned 'inner mother' onto, so we can "see" it.

The classic way this projection plays out in the United States is in the phenomena of men attracted to imagery of big-breasted women. It's been observed by many how breast imagery, breast-feeding icons, speak to the unconscious desire for nurturing in men.

Some of the appeal of big-breast imagery for men tracks back to un-met needs for SELF-nurturing, for the 'inner mother.' In this way when men look at women, they can be playing the game of, "Are you my mother?"

Commercial advertisements exploit our deficit of inner-nurturing by using sex to sell. Some ads are more explicit in selling the benefit of mothering available in their product. As was predicted decades ago, sex is now being used to sell even food, like yogurt and chocolate, especially to women. This is the paradox of selling healthy, functional 'inner mothering' to women even to mothers!

R~L sides as how we face the 3D world

Are you facing the 3D world 100% with both your right and left sides? This is not something you know with your rational mind. The answer to this is in your habit body, in your subconscious. Measuring via K-testing becomes so useful here, the easy way to access subconscious info so the rational mind can make choices about it.

Our legs and feet represent how we go forward into the 3D world. How each of us faces the outer world is colored by our capacities on both sides. Naturally one side will be stronger than the other, at least slightly. Each of us faces our world with a unique balance of yin-YANG. It's okay to "put your best foot forward." These expressions can easily be measured, quantified and altered using K-testing. If you get stuck, give me a call.

NEW Energy Anatomy

R~L hip & leg contrast

Our Left hip and leg represent our capacity to step forward and accept-receive emotional support and to get our own needs met.

Another way of saying this is, our left hip and leg represent how easy it is for us to support our own needs in our own Habit Body, immune system, inner child. This is our gratitude side.

Our Right hip and leg is our capacity to step forward and serve the goals and projects of ourselves and others. how we support ourselves out in the world and including giving to others. This is our generosity side. How easy is it for me to move forward on my goals in the 3D world? What am I willing to fight for?

When a person is aligned with their own goals and dreams; and in turn, these are aligned with the highest good of all concerned, with truly human values, then it's easy to stride forward confidently into the world anticipating success. This is the feeling of, "I am on a sure path of success" (J-Rism).

Question for self-study R~L

- How harmonious are my right and left foot with each other, on a scale of 1-10?
- How harmonious are my right and left knees with each other?

- How harmonious are my right and left hips?

- How harmonious are my right and left ovaries?

- How harmonious are my right and left kidneys?

- How harmonious are my right and left digestive organs?

- How harmonious are my right and left lungs?

In the head it switches. It's no longer right and left but it's QUADRANTS, how harmonious are all for quadrants?

R~L as two halves of abundance & prosperity

Again, the right side of our body expresses our YANG (Sun) capacities while our left side expresses our yin (Moon) capacities. Consider now if your successes in life so far have more the quality of the Moon or of the Sun? Perhaps of both?

Our EXPERIENCE of abundance is not the same on the R~L sides of our body. YANG success does not satisfy yin needs; yin successes mean little to our YANG side. This is at the heart of why workaholics can make piles of money and yet feel personally unfulfilled; and, why stay-at-home-moms are prone to getting the "housewife blues."

Abundance on the right side feels like this

You are likely to perceive abundance on your right side as confidence, perceived ability and enthusiasm to go out into the world to express, reach out for, step into, and manifest, according to your values. Its endgame is manifestation and accomplishment in the outer world.

Abundance on the left side feels like this

You are likely to perceive abundance on your left side as satisfaction, as things arranged as to meet your own needs, as healthy boundaries between you and other people you know. Feeling safe to allow others to touch

NEW Energy Anatomy

into you and ability to say "yes" or "no" *easily* to what they offer you. Perceived ability to get your own needs met and that people you know, the world and your own Divinity have good things for you, if you ask for them. That's the endgame of left-side, abundance in your inner world.

Extraverted cultures have much less language for and understanding of satisfaction on the left side. Extraverts benefit from contemplating the "koans" of "smiling energy" and "kidney yin."

Q: Can I measure and raise my abundance on my right and left sides?

A: Absolutely. Go at it as Rumi recommends. To paraphrase Rumi, he says it doesn't work to go at love or abundance or any positive quality *directly*. If we do, we are going to be applying our ego, our willpower; and often, extraverted strategies to achieve introverted, left-sided satisfactions.

What does work and what the Angels have set up for us to do—for those who choose to—is to work on our blocks to abundance, love and satisfaction.

For any positive quality you can name, it can be further unblocked and strengthened. You don't have to know how—you only have to ask ~ Maryann Castellanos.

Before a low measurement, a low number can be raised, a baseline measurement must be established; a beginning place, a place to start.

A scale of 1-10 seems the most convenient. This also permits subjective measures (conscious self opinion only, the cerebral nervous system only) which encourages people who do not yet test to engage and guess.

What works in any series of internal measurements is to always work with the lowest number. Use any tools in your Toolbox. If you get stuck, give me a call at the phone number on my websites.

R~L as "firing on both cylinders"

Feel free to experiment with the idea of each person having two "cylinders," one on your right side (YANG, masculine, Lancelot and Arthur) and one for the left side (nourishing yin, Guinever mostly).

Another possible question is, "Am I coming from a balance of my male and female energies in this moment, in what I'm about to say and do?"

Let me know what you learn about yourself!

R~L as younger and old in the our psyche

Our right YANG side is our younger side in consciousness. It is somewhat less mature in experience and less wise in experience than our left side. The United States is a wonderful example of this. From the 1700s until WW II, the U.S. was built on the strength of young energies and especially salesmanship, a prime extraverted expression. Naturally then, the deficits of the U.S. are mostly on the left side: diabetes, little thought beyond the present moment, haphazard relationships, and so on.

The reality of our right side as younger and left side as older will only become fully apparent when we later talk about Lancelot and Arthur on the right side and Guinever and Merlin on our left side.

NEW Energy Anatomy

R~L as lion & lamb

The New Testament mention of "the lion and the lamb will lay down together" also suggests the peace and harmony possible when our right and left sides, our YANG and yin capacities, are cooperative and peaceful.

Dg – 12 lion lamb

R~L as two halves of seeing

Generally to explore any positive quality, it's helpful to chunk it down into its expressions RIGHT~left.

On the Right is our capacity to see out into, our willingness to see out and beyond our own personal field.

On the Left is our capacity to be seen, to allow ourselves to be seen, to allow others to see us—especially emotionally. It's on our left that we expose ourselves to view, to the scrutiny of others.

Want to take these two distinctions further? Check out the Inner Court in New View Six.

R~L as healthy "yes" and healthy "no"

One place to find the healthy masculine is in a healthy "yes!" Identifying a positive vision, gathering support and arranging for consensus.

One place to find the healthy feminine is in a healthy "no." Notice no exclamation point, simply saying no to what you do not want.

R~L as two halves of receptivity

Most mysterious of all positive qualities in any extraverted culture is receptivity. To explore any positive quality, it's helpful to chunk it down into its expressions RIGHT~left.

Until someone suggests better language, what seems to work is to look at receptivity on the right as willingness to give to others. This is summarized wonderfully in John-Roger's Armor of the Spiritual Warrior; which includes, "touching to others with all of our goodness." Marvelous.

On our Left is our capacity to give; in other words, to receive from others. Now we have to turn "touching to others with all of our goodness" around: Allowing others to touch to us with all of their goodness.

But Wait! There's more! Since so many self-healers begin as very co-dependent, we don't wish to open ourselves recklessly to anyone who wishes to touch us in any way. So we revise the inverse of J-R's phrase this way: Allowing other people we know, the world and spirit, to touch to us with all goodness possible and permitted, keeping clear our mutually healthy boundaries, on all levels.

Want to take these two distinctions further? Check out the Inner Court in New View Six.

Much more on R~L in Heart Psychology

There is so much to say on right and left re the Pericardium meridian, we have put it into another topic called Heart Psychology. See HealingToolbox.org for an

NEW Energy Anatomy

intro article. Hopefully a book will come forth when a co-author shows up.

Kidney YANG is activated by giving in generosity. Kidney yin is activated by receiving in gratitude.

Our pericardium meridian asks us, Can you give generously from your right-sided energies? and, can you accept offers of assistance graciously with your left-sided energies?

Our body heals from right to left

In Homeopathy students are introduced to Herring's Law of Cure, a rule of thumb; which observes, patients heal from the head down, from inside to outside and in the reverse order symptoms appeared in.

We can add to this now: the body tends to heal from right to left.

Q: WHY does the body tend to heal from the top down and right to left?

A: The answer has to do with Light and Dark and the sunny and shady sides of the mountain, above. All true healing, at some level, is about redeeming part so our body stuck in too-slow frequencies and rhythms. We redeem these by raising their vibration, frequency, rhythm or all three.

In visual terms this is analogous to bringing light to our dark places. Where does Light come from? It comes from above us, over our heads and it tends to come into the body from the right YANG side towards the dimmer yin left side.

Our sunny YANG side is more aligned with these: our rational mind-soul-choice and the Father in Heaven. Our shady yin side is more aligned with our inner child, reactivity and our Mother God in Creation. We need BOTH of these; neither is superior to the other.

Our right side also tends to heal first because in the West, we are awake and aware to our right side more than to our left side. We are out of balance this way.

Further, if we enjoy prayer, frequencies of Love, Light and Angels come in to the right side of individuals and then across to the left side of the body. The initial "impact" is to the right side; the left side gets what's left over—and this contributes to feeling cheated unless you are thoro in bringing Love, Light and Angels ALL THE WAY ACROSS to your left side; likewise, all the way down to your feet and toenails

Strokes and R~L imbalances

Too great a contrast between your right and left sides is not healthy. You don't want either side much stronger and dominant over the other side. They are supposed to work together as a team. If one side gets massively ahead of the other in strength, this increases the possibility of a future stroke. Many strokes appear to be the consequence of conflict between R~L sides of the body. The winner is the one left standing. Tendencies towards this imbalance can be worked out with Solution-Based Self-Healing.

When R~L are mixed up: mixed dominance

Quietly in the 1950s and 1960s, things children love to do were validated as healthy developmentally. Further, supposedly lost learning faculties in children with learning difficulties, were redeemed by prescribing sensory integration exercises, kinesthetic "games" like "log rolling," (carefully rolling children along a carpeted floor),

NEW Energy Anatomy

"making burritos" (rolling children up inside a blanket, then unrolling them) and crawling thru cloth tunnels. See further discussion of dyslexia, cross-dominant patterns, remedial issues and the Dennisons in both *You Have Three Selves*, vol. 1, and *The Inner Court, Close-up of the Habit Body*.

Q: Is their a best-case dominance of hands, feet and so on?

A: Yes, the Waldorf Extra Lesson remedial teachers have determined the most beneficial "wiring" of our etheric body is to have all right-sided dominance. That means you would prefer to use your right ear, right eye, right hand and right foot. Mixed dominance is any variation from this. I have yet to meet a single person who is completely right side dominant. All of us seem to be working to get our right and left sides in balance; also, top to bottom; also, front to back. Touch for Health has the most effective front to back balancing pose I know of.

Our culture is out of whack RIGHT~*left*

Richard D. Wolff, an economics professor (www.democracyatwork.info) says our culture is out of balance. He says in the mainstream, Washington D.C. And Wall Street, all attention has been shifted to competition. All goals of every kind are proposed to be met thru marketplace competition.

Let's rephrase that in NEW Energy Anatomy terms: all economic and marketplace goals will be achieved only and exclusively thru the right-sided approach to human life, thru Lancelot and King Arthur.

Wolff points out how unlikely this approach is to be successful. He points out when the U.S. had its greatest periods of growth, a balance of competitive and nurturing expressions and programs was present; also, the income equality was the most equal it has ever been. When Civil Rights and Aid for Women and Infant Children and Planned Parenthood education was funded, the whole economy responded.

Compare that to the current Gilded Age when every economic and political goal is proposed to be funded by removing all nurturing and social support of every kind; that is, "killing" the left side.

In Health Intuitive terms, when the right side attacks the left side with this kind of vehemence, this is what leads to the acute physical body symptom called stroke.

A caricature of RIGHT~left

Practical imagery here may be why some people have anger issues and others have weak assimilation issues; in caricature, that's how right and left side issues present in people, if we look at just the feeling level, between belly button and below heart, on the level of Guinever and Lancelot—explained in View SIX.

R~L as the two fears of the psoas muscles

Finally in terms of converging R~L sides back into Oneness—what can we say?

One thing to say is the topic is deep and highly connected with your own courage to choose intimacy over fear. To unite R~L sides we somewhat heal our splits top to bottom in the body. One of the last places we converge R~L is in the pelvic floor where we have opportunity to acknowledge the two fears of the psoas muscles.

On the right side, our fear of either being killed, destroyed, eaten up, consumed—and losing our physical identity and physical self esteem that way.

NEW Energy Anatomy

On the left, our fear of being utterly and completely abandoned and alone—losing all sense of our self in relationship to other people—losing our identify and self-concept that way. This kind of loss is well-portrayed in the Tom Hanks "Castaway" movie.

R~L as two different upward spirals

Sooner or later in paying attention to your R~L sides you are likely to notice what they are doing is easily characterized by spirals. Classically, either the spiral is going up, going down or it's stuck. Spirals can change day to day and hour by hour so don't take any one reading too seriously.

What you *might* find on your left side, when your left side spiral is healthy, is simple and uncomplicated, simple, like the pleasure of moving your body to music, the pleasure of feeling your needs met, energy coming up from the body in lovely, safe gentle expressions.

When your right side spiral is healthy, what you *might* find on your right side, is a more complex action. This is akin to the Search for the Grail. The masculine recognizes the active quality of Spirit. The mature masculine, on the right side, can relax its ego and direct its gaze UP to the SOURCE of energy coming down. This is the timeless image of looking up to the Grail. The Grail is an archetype of looking up to receive what is coming down from Above. The masculine looks UP to this image, accepting and loving the attention and energy coming down from God now.

Finally, kidney yin, on our left side, from the neck down, has some as-yet-unclear connection with the right brain hemisphere. Kidney YANG, on right left side, from the neck down, has some as-yet-unclear connection with the left brain hemisphere.

R~L as goals and needs

Our body tells us goals and needs are different.

In speaking with a client the other day, I realized he and many people I know struggle with a confusion between goals and needs. We think they are the same. They are not the same. Our own body clarifies how goals and needs are two different things.

We have goals on our right side

In our body, goals align with our right, YANG side. Our right side is our YANG side, the sunny side of the hill, our Arnold Schwarzenegger side, our active "go for it" side.

This is the side of liver and gallbladder (pirates and ninjas) and kidney YANG. It's the side of Lancelot and King Arthur in Arthurian Legend. Our capacity for giving generously comes from the right pericardium meridian, down the inside of the right arm, towards the world.

Goals are outer, in the 3D world, about progress, increase, material abundance, greater resources.

Conclusion: Our body tells us goals are about fulfillment in the outer world.

Needs are on our left side

In contrast to this needs are on our left side. The left side of our body is our YIN side, the shady side of the hill, our Ingrid Bergman-Judy Garland side, our passive, subjunctive and "at-effect" side, our "lady-in-waiting" side, arranging things among her allies and enemies in the kingdom, so that down the line, she gets her own needs met.

NEW Energy Anatomy

This is the side of stomach, pancreas, spleen and kidney yin. It's the side of Guinever and Merlin in Arthurian Legend. Our capacity for receiving in gratitude comes from the left pericardium meridian, down the inside of the left arm, towards the world. Think Meryl Streep.

Conclusion: Our body tells us needs are about **fulfillment** in our inner world.

English language tracks us towards goals

In writing my own needs further below, I realize English is a language of goals—not needs. If you know a language better suited to expressing needs, please make a comment on this article.

This means, in English, needs will always sound weaker, less important and less interesting than goals.

Sound familiar, women? This line of thought takes us into how paternalism and dominator thinking dominates conventional mainstream English.

Dreams as needs

"Goals" has also taken over for "dreams" in many respects as well. When we talk about the American Dream, we always mean a single-family-dwelling and some variation on a nuclear-family pattern.

But what about the American Dream of women's equality in the workplace, home and bedroom?

What about the American Dream of William Penn, founder of the state of Pennsylvania, for a land of agricultural peace, economic prosperity and religious freedom?

What about the American Dream for meaningful work in

large intentional communities of the late 1800s and 1970s and 1980s?

What about the French dream of Equality, Liberty and Fraternity?

What about the American Dream of preserving ecological, environmental and planetary integrity? Need I go on?

In all of these above we are voicing dreams of fulfillment. For those who like these dreams, hey are needs.

It's plenty clear in the Industrial West at least, "dreams" have been hijacked to a variable extent by language geared to smaller-minded, more narrow-minded corporate consumer interests.

Wants or needs?

Google has many articles clarifying the difference between wants and needs; this aspect of the discussion is already well-covered. In brief, and in the present context, if you don't get your needs met, you start dying inside, especially on your left side.

If you don't get your wants met, this dying does not occur; or at least, you only die from the neck up. If you don't get your needs met, you begin dying from the neck down.

A way to clarify your fulfillment needs

Goals need no discussion. Every red-blooded American has goals, what they want in the 3D world, and can tell you what they are. What they can NOT tell you is their needs, on the left side.

NEW Energy Anatomy

Needs PACMES

Perhaps the simplest way to clarify your fulfillment needs is to fill in the blanks on a PACMES grid. PACME abbreviates the Light & Sound Map of Creation, Spiritual Geography 101:

P stands for Physical ~ or Cellular

A stands for Astral ~ or Imaginal, likes and dislikes, polarities, ambition

C stands for Causal ~ or Emotional

M stands for Mental

E stands for Etheric ~ or Mythological, super heroes and archetypes, scripts we live by

S stands for Spiritual, Soul and Above, the Home Office for all souls now here in 3D

So you fill in a grid to clarify your fulfillment needs. Here are mine for today:

P ~ Exercising with an exercise buddy. Continue providing top nutrition to my body. Deep sleep. Gardening with edible foods, reclaiming "lost" land. Time to do spiritual exercises. Travel as necessary and useful to help others help themselves at a higher rate.

A ~ Finding the others who want to build new sustainable intentional communities. Participate in more and better Dances of Universal Peace! More Waldorf-methods schools.

C ~ Loving relations with clients and people wherever I am NOW. Being useful for those in need of clarifying their own fulfillment needs. Learning how to ground my emotional self more fully. More practice with

Compassionate (nonviolent) Communication, strengthening my habits of listening first for people's feelings and needs before I speak.

M ~ Less writing replaced with more clients and more community-building! Being useful for those in need of energy detective work or who wish to learn it with 'God as their Partner.'

E ~ More alignment and attunement with the inner archetypes of health, wealth and happiness; abundance, riches and prosperity; loving, caring and sharing; touching to each other with all of our gifts; keeping clear our mutually healthy boundaries between us. Clearing blocks and obstacles in the unconscious towards inner experience of inner Love, Light, Sound and Laugher.

S ~ Clearing misperceptions about myself, other people, the world and how easy it is to connect with my own Divinity.

That's my list today. What may be missing for many people is some sexuality needs. Feel free to add those to you list.

We can be split-off from our needs by "towards" and "away"

Find discussion in NLP in this vein:

People are motivated to move either towards or away from things, people, situations. People who only motivate themselves with "toward" (goals) may never get around to doing the nagging unpleasant things necessary to make their life better.

People who only motivate themselves with "away" thinking (avoiding pain), may never set new goals for themselves until their life is in a negative crisis.

NEW Energy Anatomy

The above yields many useful insights. Most people do not need help in doing things that are pleasant. Believe it or not; tho, some people experience setting goals and making To Do lists as extremely painful, fearful and overwhelming.

Expanded for clarity from
http://www.transformdestiny.com/nlp-guide/nlp-motivation-strategies.asp

"Towards" and "away" figure into the present discussion this way. It's very common to have towards goals on the right side of your body: I want a million dollars, I want a spouse, write a book, etc. BUT to have only away goals on the left side of the body: a pain-free life, no debts, less stress.

The problem with this split is even if you get all your away goals met, you only have nothing, you still have no personal, unique-to-you, creative fulfillment. This takes us back to dreams and is why so many goal-setting processes begin with giving people permission to dream and get in touch with their inner six year old who had a dream of becoming a fireman or a nurse.

More general characterizations of right and left

Left side: Welcome and receive support from people, environment and the Universe. Allow another to assist me to be successful.

Right side: Support others, reach out to others and the world for success.

FAQs

Q: Why are their no financial items on your list?

A: $$$ is on the right side goals. From the perspective

of the left side, $$$ is only a means to an end. The need is the inner experience you wish to have--when you do make all the money you wish to make.

Needs are primarily inner experiences

Needs are primarily inner experiences. That's why we are so weak on them here in what's left of the United States. We are out of balance with identifying what inner experiences we are after. We have very few leaders here. Martin Luther King was a leader here. As someone pointed out, Dr. King gave the "I have a dream speech," not the, "I have a plan" speech. This is a key--what's your dream?

Part of our split-off-ness from our own healthy needs is how we are somewhat one-sidedly pursuing OUTER goals and have neglected our inner needs, what we might call fulfillment needs. You CAN reclaim these and achieve a better right-left balance.

To Learn More

1) Values, Needs, Wants, and Goal Setting Essentials [this is not a body-based approach but has attractive diagrams and brings in values]

http://cbirgen.wikispaces.com/file/view/Values_Needs_Wants_and_Goal_Setting_Essentials_Advanced_Info_Sheet_7.17.2.F1.pdf

2) MuseInks: Goals vs. Needs [for novelists and scriptwriters to compose character and craft motivation]

museinks.blogspot.com/2008/09/goals-vs-needs.html

NEW Energy Anatomy

Final words on R~L

Our R~L sides hold much information, up to and including the mythological level.

One aspect of this is the common idea of extraverted and introverted thinking.

Without writing another book, we can point out a polarity of beliefs extraverts and introverts express.

Extraverts often think, I'm spiritual because of what I DO.

Introverts often think, I'm spiritual because of what I feel and think on the inside, according to my values; and ultimately, my alignment.

Right here may be some insights on the DO and BE discussion; am I a human *doing* or a human *being*? Maybe both are good; as in the immortal words of Frank Sinatra, "Do, Be, Do, Be, Do!"

Summary of R~L

YANG on right side of body, below the neck, yin on left side below the neck.

Yin on front side of body, below the neck, YANG on back side.

Self-esteem on the front of the body (CV, Sea of Yin).

Self-concept on the back of body (GV, Sea of YANG)

Healthy Self-esteem + healthy self-concept = healthy self-confidence.

The Prayer of right and left

It's easy for me to feel the Light moving thru my right side and out into the world, touching to other people.

~ New view TWO ~

The human hourglass

Our two brains, ENS and CNS, are upstairs and downstairs in the human psyche.

We'll pose a question here you may wish to return to. Do you live more upstairs or downstairs in your psyche in any given day?

We are going to expand on Caroline Myss' (pronounced "Mace") idea of the human hour glass, that human energy is organized top and bottom in the body. We're going to suggest why the diaphragm muscle divides these two and why it makes sense we have TWO nervous systems; our two minds--and this is a good thing! The following mixes Myss' ideas with those of Maryann Castellanos and some of my own.

The human psyche has magnetic properties; specifically, humans have a north and south pole. Our diaphragm muscle divides these polarities top and bottom.

The practical significance of having two magnetic poles is embodied in our two nervous systems. One is the enteric (gut) nervous system. It lives in our south pole. The other is our cerebral (brain, spinal cord and spinal nerves) nervous system. It lives in our north pole.

This simple idea can replace the older, more confusing terms: sympathetic and parasympathetic nervous systems.

Caroline Myss' hourglass image

In Caroline Myss's 12 CD kit, *The Science of Medical Intuition* (Sounds True, 2002), and in *Invisible Acts of Power* she talks about the hourglass form.

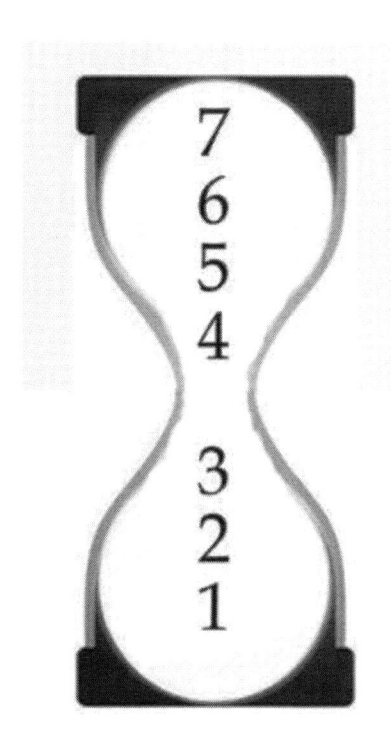

Going from bottom up, she describes the heart chakra as the first center in our top north pole. If we number our etheric centers 1-7, we then have diagram 13.

Combining Myss' idea with what Maryann Castellanos has shown me, the narrow waist in the hourglass image is more precisely the diaphragm muscle, the large dome-shaped muscle we use for breathing. Above the diaphragm is the system of heart, throat, brow and crown. Below the heart is the system of centers, belly, sacral and root. These three lower centers approximate the physical body, speaking energetically.

dg-13 (hg1-7)

Different tempos above and below

The hourglass image suggests the possibility of different tempos top and bottom in the human psyche; and this is so.

Myss observes in the bottom half of our hourglass, we are "linear and sequential." This is the slower tempo. Life

NEW Energy Anatomy

situations are processed one by one and sequentially. The manner in which the gastrointestinal tract processes food illustrates this preference for the linear and the sequential. Myss suggests not only food but also emotional experiences are processed this way below the heart.

Above the heart, Myss says linear sequential processing is much less a factor. We can change time, make new appointments, cancel old ones; we can change time. We have the capacity to think and move at the speed of light. In the heart and above, we can do this; we are "holographic" Myss says. Above the diaphragm, our etheric centers are more blended than below the diaphragm; they're more of a team.

In childhood, specifically before puberty, when the bottom half of the hourglass predominates, body, imagination and feelings are all converged, perceived as similar and the same.

Myss' characterization of how things need to happen in the lower half of the hourglass tells us much about how the basic self and children want to, need to, experience life and how they process their disturbances. Young children and the b/s in everyone needs things to happen in a predictable orderly sequence, otherwise they have a difficult time learning, processing hurt and evolving.

In this the lower half of the hourglass we are akin to plants. A flower blossom's opening is tied to a sequence of necessary events in time: First there is spring thaw, then moisture and warmth, then leaf-leaf-leaf, bud--and if conditions are right--you get a blossom.

In the top half of the hourglass, in our head, in great contrast, the rational mind can start with an image of a blossom and work our way backwards to the seed. Indeed, the c/s becomes bored if everything happens too predictably. It likes surprises and deviations from routine.

This ends Caroline's Myss' contribution to this topic, known to me. Corrections and clarifications are invited.

Enteric and Cerebral Nervous systems (NS)

Hourglass imagery is useful to characterize our two nervous systems. We have two concentrations of nerve tissue in our body. One concentration above in the brain, a second concentration of nerve tissues below in our "gut." This suggests the human being has brains in two places—and this is so. We have two distinct nervous systems and BOTH of them are intelligent.

One nervous system, composed of nerve tissue, is in your "gut," the enteric nervous system (ENS). You also see it termed "mesenteric nervous system;" and, "abdominal brain." Your "gut brain" is located primarily below your diaphragm muscle in the nerve tissues of the omentum, stomach, pancreas, spleen, part of the small intestine, esophagus and tongue.

Hologram thinking (multi-tasking)

Linear thinking (one thing at a time)

The omentum is by far the least known anatomical part in this list. It is the flap of nerve tissue overhanging the stomach and adjacent organs as in the image. The experience of being "punched in the gut"

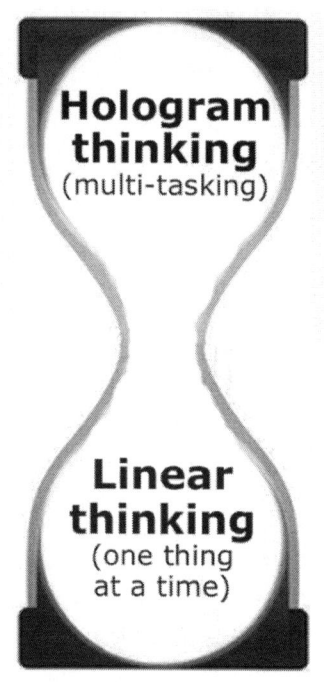

Dg-15 holo-linear

and "butterflies in the stomach" originate solely from the omentum, so, it's a big part of the gut brain.

Your second nervous system is in your "head," your cerebral nervous system (CNS). It too is composed of

NEW Energy Anatomy

nerve tissue, located primarily in your spinal cord, brain and the nerves radiating out from the spine.

Find out much more about your two nervous systems in *You Have Three Selves*, Vol. 1 and in many articles at my sites.

In physiologic terms, energetic strength is Coherence, Integration and Alignment--the new CIA--between our two nervous systems, our two brains.

The more CIA we are, the more humans function as One Whole instead of as Two Minds. Therefore, unresolved issues, any issue on which we are "of two minds," keeps us OUT of integration and depletes our energetic strength.

Q: You mean, the more integrated we are top and bottom, the fewer inner barriers we have and the greater our potential vitality?

A: Yup, that about sums it up.

In the 1940s Wilhelm Reich correlated personality disturbances with differences in energetic charge in the physical body. He noticed not only striking differences between different individuals as to charge in the body; but also, differences in charge within individuals, between the half of the body above the diaphragm muscle and the half of the body below the diaphragm. Either half could be undercharged; either could be overcharged and virtually every permutation can be observed in people. In turn these patterns of over and undercharge correlate with personality expressions. Thru study, Reich grew "new eyes" to see; for instance, a person who was overcharged above the diaphragm muscle and who; at the same time, was also weak below the diaphragm muscle. This defined for Reich the classic "neurotic" pattern, something still useful today, for those interested in reading body language.

A chicken-and-egg question arises here: is low energy below the diaphragm the cause of anatomies below the diaphragm, "skinny legs and all"? Or do the skinny legs come first and then the depleted energy? Answers are individual here.

Reich describes the patterns he found simply and clearly in his forgotten yet surprisingly readable and cogent, *Character Analysis* (1948).

Our cerebral nervous system (CNS) and enteric nervous system (ENS) are "upstairs" & "downstairs" in our physical body.

ENS-CNS as self-esteem and self-concept

Self-esteem is the health of our feeling-desire & willingness in our gut brain, the ENS.

Self-esteem is the health of our feeling-desire & willingness in our gut brain, the ENS.

Self-concept is the health of how we think about our self on all levels in our head brain, the CNS.

Puberty is well-described as the migration of the locus of control from the lower to the upper half of the human hourglass.

Prior to puberty, we are given opportunities to develop self-esteem in our habit body.

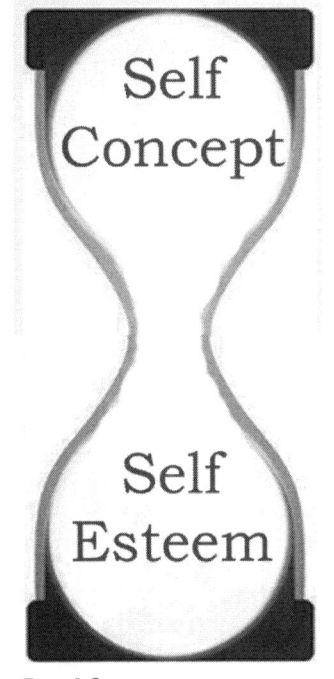

Dg-16 sc-se

After puberty, we are given opportunity to develop and exercise self-concept in our rational thinking.

NEW Energy Anatomy

One nervous system dominates in the adult hourglass

Our two nervous systems locate our two minds. As MBTI makes clear, both feeling and thinking are rational ways to evaluate and make decisions. Yet, "A man cannot serve two masters." One of these rational approaches dominates and is preferred in each individual.

Some people are rational feeling dominant. They make decisions rationally based on how two choices feel to them. This is a good way to evaluate choices and make decisions. For them thinking is their non-preferred mode. This arrangement is not easy to diagram.

For about 80% of us in the West, we are rational thinking dominant. We compare two choices using thinking. This is another good way to evaluate choices and make decisions. For us feeling is the non-preferred mode. This arrangement is easy to diagram:

Loving and feeling connect top and bottom

Consider how the narrow waist between top and bottom can be likened to an energetic bottleneck. Indeed, we are all working towards greater integration of top and bottom, ENS & CNS, conscious self and habit body.

Our top-bottom integration is the most significant integration of all our energetic polarities.

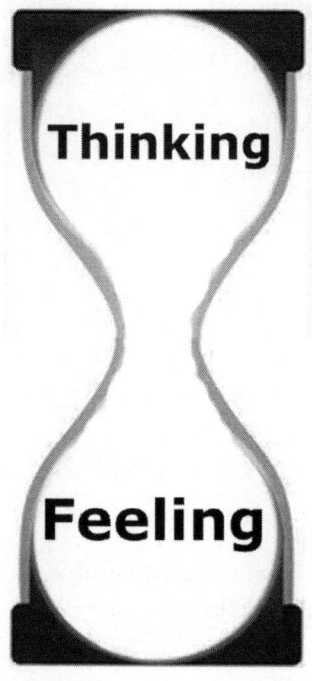

Dg-18 T-F

Each 3D embodiment is opportunity to increase our integration.

Q: If 100% top bottom integration is optimal, what is average now?

A: A good research project! Preliminary indications suggest 50% top-bottom integration is likely way above average at this time.

As MBTI teaches, our rational process can be either thinking (cerebral) or feeling (enteric). Still where the center of gravity for each of these capacities appears to remain stable across this variation.

You have two minds and this is a good thing

Maryann Castellanos says the ultimate destiny of ENS and CNS is not to become a big mush pile. Each must retain their own character. Love and feeling is what enables them to communicate across barriers, bottlenecks and hurts.

Which would you rather have? One single arm coming out of the middle of your chest; or, a separate right and left hand on opposite sides of your body? I'm sure you can imagine many advantages to having two hands, like holding a baby, juggling, steering a bicycle, etc.

How about one single, central leg, would you prefer that over two legs bilaterally?

We have two brain hemispheres for very similar reasons.

Acknowledging two NSs permits discussion of dynamics and interplay between mind and emotions, while staying anchored in terms of the body. Like the Three Selves, ENS and CNS is a leap forward in taking psychology out of the abstract, connecting it into the body, where we can work

NEW Energy Anatomy

with invisible energy most conveniently.

Objections to "the human psyche has two poles"

Q: Wait, I do the same things with the top half of my body as I do with my bottom half. They both have muscles, bones and circulate blood.

A: True. How about this tho: do you think, form images and solve problems primarily with your feet and legs? Do you primarily digest and circulate food and fluids for digestion, assimilation and excretion in your head or with your arms and hands? Which part of you enables you to move quickly to catch the bus in the morning? Which part of you do you use to do an algebra problem?

The human energy body and psyche has significant polarity and this is crucial to the NEW energy anatomy.

The human cell has magnetic poles

A new insight on human cells also exists, thanks to Maryann Castellanos. According to her clairvoyant observations, human cells have N and S poles.

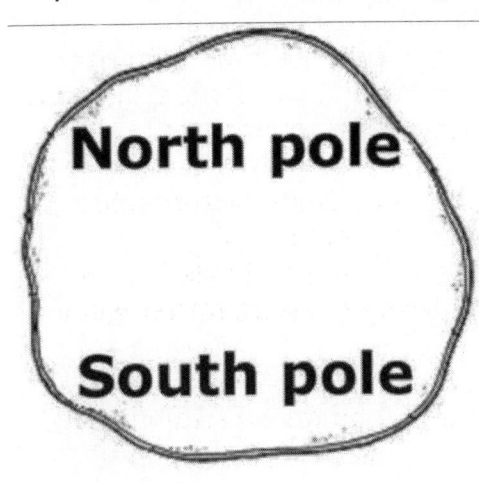

Dg-19 cell N-S

Q: What are the north and south poles oriented to?

A: No idea yet. This is preliminary basic research. Time for you to get involved!

The apparent fact of magnetic polarity in

112

human cells is not reported in conventional science. North and south poles are not visible thru any microscope yet devised. Blood cells are famously round with no distinguishing north and south features. Google images will show you many drawings of "human cells" none of them with north and south poles.

That human cells have polarity would be news and a great uncovery. Complicating this uncovery further, she says cell polarity is much less visible in plant and animal cells suggesting animals and plants have much less polarity than human beings are capable of. Cell polarity may in fact be a unique energetic aspect of human cell anatomy.

Maryann's concept of energetic strength is closely related to her observations here. The better each cell, all cells, can communicate between top and bottom, the more cellular vitality exists.

The evidence here is only clairvoyant observations and inferential so far. The Earth demonstrates its poles in how most of the rigid land mass lies in the north, more of the thinking quality; while the south, is more characterized by water, more of the feeling nature, an observation from Waldorf-method geography.

Above we suggest each person has North and South poles. The heart and liver not only have north and south poles in my experience but also four quadrants, something I learned from Medical Intuitive, Carol Ritberger. Moving on down to smaller structures, its reasonable to explore how poles could exist MICROscopically for each cell, even if invisible in their physical structure. After al, these must be rather weak fields.

It is reasonable to explore and look for polarity in each part, down to the cell level.

NEW Energy Anatomy

Preferences Right~Left, Top~Bottom

Alert readers will already be composing their own variations on the above material. I celebrate that; and, do you best to stay aligned with Love, Light and Angels.

The analytical approach used here has a serious limitation; it can reach no higher than the mind. Since you as soul are much more than mind, remember to keep going.

Enteric dominance is a preference for the Inner Court in the gut: gut brain perceptions.

Within the preference for the gut brain can be a preference for either the right or left side of the gut brain.

Right side of the gut brain, Lancelot and King Arthur, liver-gall bladder.

Left side of the gut brain, Guinever and Merlin, stomach, pancreas, spleen.

The fast way to see this is to ask about which side of the body you have more physical issues on. That's usually the weak side. You prefer using the other side.

Q: What does "prefer" mean here?

A: "Prefer" and "strong" here suggest which side they have more tools and ability to modulate. The weak side will be the side where you have fewer tools and ability to moderate charge. That's why it's weak. That's why your attention is drawn to your weak side, to strengthen your Tools That Heal and strategies on that side.

Cerebral dominance is a preference for less sensory, more abstract perceptions. Within this can be found preference for capacities in either the front or back of the head.

Preference for front or back in the head will show up--somehow--in either right or left side of the gut brain.

The practical picture here may be why some people have anger issues and others have weak assimilation issues; in caricature, that's how right and left side present.

Strength and ability in the front half of the brain, will show up as strength on the right side of the gut brain, Lancelot and King Arthur (liver-gall bladder).

Strength and ability in the rear half of the brain, will show up as strength on the left side of the gut brain, Guinever and Merlin (stomach-pancreas-spleen).

Top and bottom as see-saw, as teeter-totter

The hourglass image is one way to see into the polarity of top and bottom in human energy. Another image is the see-saw or teeter totter, as one side goes up, the other must go down; also, to play the game, both sides are moving towards balance, equal weights on both ends.

In the process of balancing out our unresolved disturbances, I'm aware my soul, perhaps all souls, do something that a see-saw depicts very clearly.

If we look at individual development on a timeline, the picture is often like this, in the past we have some extreme behavior that is too heavy and weighing down that end of the see-saw way too much. That particular expression we learned is excessive. It really needs to be brought back into balance. How to create balance?

Well, why not put an equal weight on the other end of the see-saw?

This is what the soul does in balancing qualities inside itself.

NEW Energy Anatomy

If in the past the soul has expressed in an isolated, introverted way, perhaps living in nunneries and monasteries for multiple lifetimes, it could be useful to choose a future life expression that is at the other end, at the other polarity: outgoing, social, involved with people.

These balancing acts are much easier to see in another person than in yourself. Sometimes the soul is calming down an overcharge; at other times, nurturing an undercharged, missing or collapsed expression.

Our body has time directionality. The future and present are above, the past is below. Also, the future and present are in front and the past is behind. This is part of why, in homeopathy, they say, we heal from the head down. Our oldest patterns are the most challenging to redirect.

Because our body has time aspects, top and bottom in human energy is also a see-saw: current expressions, talents and behaviors on top trying to balance old patterns, expressions and habits on the bottom.

Our rational mind tends to take what we are doing currently for granted and mostly complain about how it's not better. From a soul point of view, that you are doing ANYTHING now, the way you are doing it, is fantastic and if you commit to WHATEVER you are doing today, it will tend to balance out, upgrade, redirect and erase old habits from long ago, where you were doing the opposite of what you are doing today.

Mostly we are not aware of what we are balancing out. This is why so many teachers encourage us to do whatever we are doing with full attention and full love. This is the fastest way to balance the top-bottom see-saw.

Top and bottom as "heat rises"

Top and bottom as see-saw connects with the old health idea "heat rises" inside the body. If too much heat rises too high in the body; then, we are out of balance, a "hot head." Did you ever feel you are busy, busy, busy and at the same time not accomplishing much? The "busy busy part" is almost always experienced in us from the neck up, occasionally also in the heart area, especially if you have panic and/or palpitations due to anxiety. The "not accomplishing much part" is experienced in the lower half of the body, may be bored, inarticulate, may have sluggish digestion and/or constipation.

Hopefully these topics in energy anatomy will point you towards more communication with your own lower part.

The top-bottom phenomena of "heat rises" is easier to see in plants and trees than in people. Once you see it in plants and people, it's much more obvious this occurs in the human kingdom as well. To chunk up, in both kingdoms these are expressions of the ether body.

Annual plants that go to seed and die each year experience a very striking arc of "heat rises." Their initial activity—heat—is root development, building a base. At the end, all their energy (heat) is at the top of the plant, going into seed production. Lower leaves are often dying or dead as the plant focuses all its energy into seeds for next year.

Deciduous (not pine) trees do this as well and on a grander scale. As they age, root growth slows down and most of the tree's activity goes into new leaf growth at the top of the tree. Holding most of your energy high in the body is not good for either tree or human. As Kahlil Gibran says, sometimes "Love prunes us for our growth." Trees can be pruned to bring more energy lower in the tree. In people, Life often asks us to abandon fantasies

NEW Energy Anatomy

that have proven impractical or untrue to the expansion of our heart—no matter how attached we were to those fantasies.

Our body heals from top to bottom

In RIGHT~left we added how the body also heals from right to left to the existing observations of the homeopath, Hering, that patients heal from the head down, from inside to outside and in the reverse order symptoms appeared in. We simply wish to remind you here the body heals primarily from the top down. This has to do with the primary path of Light into and thru our psyche.

Q: Why does the body heal from top to bottom, from above downwards?

A: I was afraid you would ask that. As usual the key to growth and development, what works and what does not work, is, "Where do I feel safe" and, "What makes me comfortable?" These two determine where we spend more time and develop more capacity in our psyche.

I think it works this way. Our cells and our high self know about Love, Light and Angels. It's mostly our small "s" self in the middle, between these two, who can't make up its mind about it's alignment. So two-thirds of us is aligned with Love, Light and Angels. They come in from the right side primarily, also from directly above, 12 o'clock high. So we tend to clear up negativity from right to left and top down because that's the most-used path of Love, Light and Angels into our body.

$$v\backslash V/v$$

~ New view THREE ~

Earthly human energy is organized front and back

Without love, power alone is ruthless and reckless.

Without power love alone is anemic and sentimental ~ Unknown

Even viewing human energy front and back, several facets still present themself.

More conscious ~ more unconscious

Taking care of the outer world ~ Taking care of our own needs

"The face we turn towards the world" is indeed on the front of our body. Our self-care needs we hide on our back. In the Inner Court, in the space of imagination, the back of some characters can be seen to be black or absent or hollow. This is imagination after all. This tells us t is lacking.

Front of body: Magnetism ~ Back of body: Electricity

In TCM the conception vessel is associated with magnetism. This means seduction is more visible, and more impactful, on the front of the body. Pick up any Victoria Secret catalogue and you have in your hands an encyclopedia of seductive expressions. Notice how virtually all the poses favor the front of the body. This is where our "come hither" forces are. This ability comes

NEW Energy Anatomy

from our magnetic potential.

In TCM the governing vessel is associated with electricity. Therefore anger is more visible on the back of the body. Anger is the most visible emotion on the back of the body, the main disturbance of our electrical potential. In comic books especially, the villains are often shown from the back to highlight their electrical power and how disturbed they are.

It's often quite striking how soft New Age men in particular can, when seen from the back, be seen to harbor significant unresolved anger. Let's not be too hard of this group tho; this is deep stuff and not easy to get at.

> One way to get at both seduction and anger is thru the Inner Court, discussed further below. Inner Court members can be interviewed about seduction, anger and so on.

Feeling and willingness ~ Character and strength

The idea we look the same front and back, is an urban myth, simply an unchecked materialistic assumption, a superstition. To "fresh eyes" front and back of any individual human body present often strikingly different 'sides' of a person.

The wisdom of body-based psychotherapies accumulated in the Bioenergetics-Esalen-Rolfing era peaked in the 1960s to early 1980s. The best lay person book I know on the deeper aspects of body language is *The Body Reveals*, 2nd Ed. Ron Kurz and Hector Presiera, MD, Harper & Row 1976, 1984.

Always go for the *feeling* in your observations. You may be surprised to feel how the front side of a person has quite a different feeing than when they face directly away from you.

This is easiest to perceive if underwear is all a person wears, so try this at home or at the beach! To SEE this you have to allow the possibility; then, note the qualitative differences.

This contrast has its clearest literature in acupuncture, in discussions of central-conception vessel in front and the governing vessel in back. This lore can be usefully extended now.

These qualities are primarily unconscious in nature, not subconscious, not conscious. They are determined primarily by the Conception Vessel (CV) in front and the Governing Vessel (GV) in back. CCV in front holds our magnetic potential. GV in back holds our electrical potential. CV in front is our deepest capacity of yin. GV in back is our deepest capacity of YANG. To some extent front and back represent time: our future forward and in front of us, our past back and behind us.

>   Front of body > Conception Vessel > self-esteem

>   Back of body > Governing Vessel > self-concept

These two meridians are often dysfunctional as a pair, perhaps always. When self-esteem suffers and becomes deficient (undercharge), self-concept is liable to become exaggerated (overcharge).

As usual, down here in 3D, dysfunctional states are much more obvious, striking and interesting, than complete harmony and balance. The classic American therapeutic metaphor goes like this:

Front of body > CV > Clark Kent the weakling

The character given from the front side of the body tends

NEW Energy Anatomy

to track back to feelings good or bad. This is most noticeable on the face, but also in the belly.

These images of Clark (CV in front) and Superman (GV in back) are too similar in frequency to represent the different between CV and GV but they give you some idea of the contrasting polarity.

Back of body > GV > muscle-bound Superman in action

Impressions given from the back side of the body track back to the individual's self-concept of their strengths and in the 19th century idea of "will" in its expressions of willfulness, wontfulness, and rigidity; also, the modern idea of healthy will as willingness.

The greater the contrast in charge between these two, undercharge in front and overcharge in back, the more harmony is blocked at our core. More on this below.

Superman and Clark Kent

The classic American character dysfunction present in front an back, conception vessel and governing vessel, is artistically expressed in Clark Kent and Superman in action. Clark Kent, the 98 pound weakling, dispossessed of any manly energy, expresses the undercharged conception vessel in front. Superman in action expresses the compensating overcharge expression, on the back of the body. See a full discussion of this in Meridian Metaphors, Psychology of the meridians and major organs.

Why Superman in action in back? The GV is our capacity for healthy concentrated attention in our unconscious habit body.

Why weak Clark Kent in front? The CV vessel is our capacity for healthy relaxation in our unconscious habit body.

Hence the two sides of the body have very significant potential polarity, front & back.

The optimal function in the psyche may be as simple as this. When the two vessels are optimally functional, individuals feel confidence to match their thoughts with their feelings. John-Roger has pointed to this as a major expression of an integrated psyche.

Dysfunction in these two vessels signals lack of integration between our gut brain and our cerebral brain.

Dysfunction in the CV looks like hiding and scatter in the ENS. Lack of focus or scatter in front. Takes concentration to create a baby, all the yin and YANG forces have to come together to make new life here. How do you make a dream come true here?

Dysfunction in the GV looks like unnecessarily rigid body-role playing-emotions-beliefs in the unconscious, over-responsibility, Indiana Jones, vigilante super-heroes.

Overcharge dysfunction

Lone Ranger, Indiana Jones, over-vigilant Putting on appearances, faking it.

Undercharge dysfunction

Inferiority, unrealistic sense of End of life issues, given up,

powerlessness emotional disintegration

See a longer discussion of superheroes in *Meridian*

NEW Energy Anatomy

Metaphors, Psychology of the meridians and major organs.

\v\V/v/

~ New view FOUR ~

Laughter as anatomy lesson

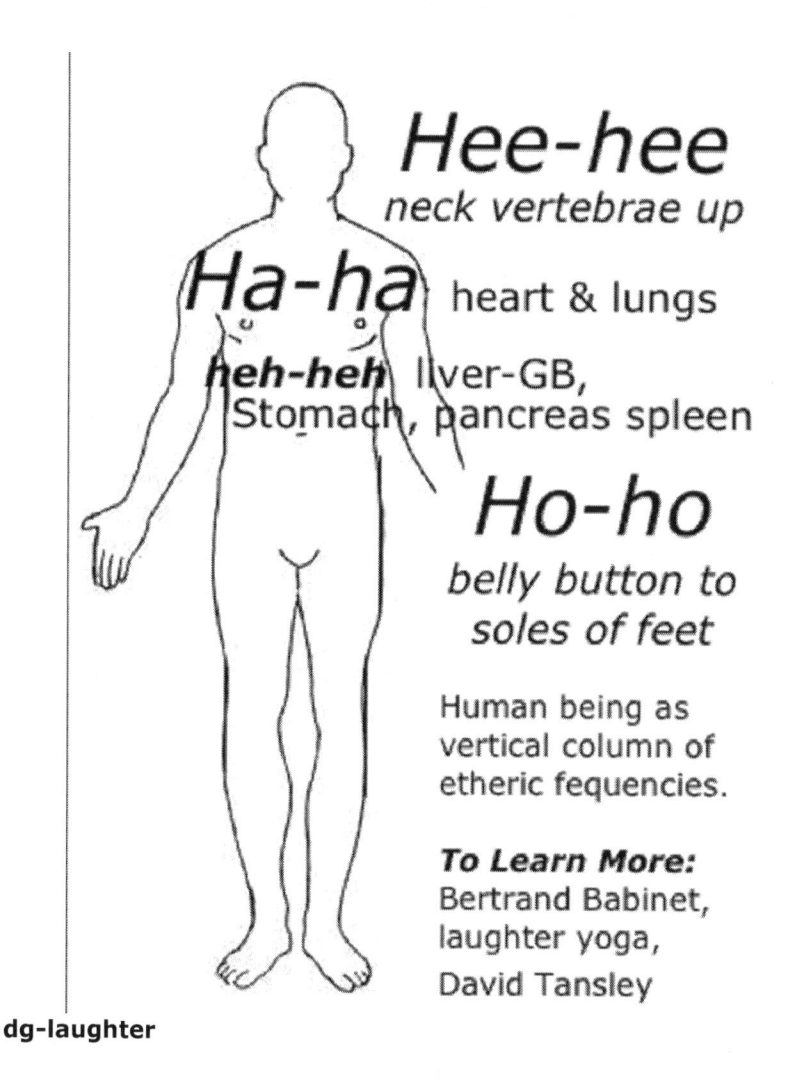

Hee-hee
neck vertebrae up

Ha-ha heart & lungs

heh-heh liver-GB, Stomach, pancreas spleen

Ho-ho
belly button to soles of feet

Human being as vertical column of etheric fequencies.

To Learn More:
Bertrand Babinet, laughter yoga, David Tansley

dg-laughter

The human etheric body is organized by frequency, top to bottom. When our basic self responds with laughter,

NEW Energy Anatomy

different laughters results, depending on the region it's responding from.

These four kinds of laughing are so common and familiar, we write them distinctly in English: Hee-hee!, Ha-ha!, heh-heh, Ho ho!.

For self-healers and anyone else interested, we can walk this backwards and use the different laughters to backtrack to which part of the body is responding. The quality of laughter becomes a reference point for which part of our anatomy is basic self is responding thru.

We can go further and use the "map" of four laughters as a locational tool to test responses in our body in four different regions.

Street corner, "laughing clubs" in India are the starting place. In the U.S. these became "laughter yoga." Mark Twain has a clear Western understanding, "...the old man laughed loud and joyously, shook up the details of his anatomy from head to foot, and ended by saying that such a laugh was money in a man's pocket, because it cut down the doctor's bills like anything," (Tom Sawyer).

The topic of four distinct laughs as reference points for four distinct body regions/frequencies in the human psyche was begun by Bertrand Babinet in the 1990s (Babinetics.com). We can infer Bertrand allowed laughter yoga to teach him four distinct vertical regions of frequency in human bodies.

He understood how the four laughs demonstrate a vertical scale of four frequency regions in all human bodies; and, how becomes a useful locational map when you are looking for invisible things such as "reactivity."

Bertrand showed how four distinct laughs comprise a convenient "map" of the body and psyche, a locational tool for locating the joys and disturbances stored in our body.

Bertrand's article on inner laughing was published in the New Day Herald, the MSIA newspaper in the 1990s but I can find no online version. Bertrand has two current online versions:

[PDF] Psychological Stress (Impact and solutions) - Babinetics

www.babinetics.com/Reports/Psychological_Stress.pdf
Copyright Bertrand Babinet, 2010.

[DOC] Secrets_to_Long_health_Life_Book_Complete_6-1-10 ...

www.babinetics.com/.../

Copyright Bertrand Babinet, 2010.

Less obvious perhaps is how laughter as anatomy and anatomy as laughter can displace many aspects of the old Theosophical-metaphysical model of chakras. As a locational tool for invisible joys and disturbances, laughter yoga is many times more accessible and useful than chakras.

While chakras remain meaningful for fully clairvoyant persons, for the rest of us, laughter is the more accessible tool. You don't have to be clairvoyant to laugh! Laughing is easier than clairvoyance!

Perhaps also not so obvious is how laughter yoga is much easier to test for and measure with muscle-testing,

NEW Energy Anatomy

compared to chakras. This is true for muscle-testing of any kind (the methods of arm-length-testing and client-controlled-kinesiology testing are now preferred).

Compared to chakras, the four frequencies of laughing are easy, natural and fun reference points because both the conscious self and basic self can perceive, work with and understand laughter very well.

The four colors of the spectrum of laughter

High frequency (conscious)

Hee, hee, hee!

Cervical spine region up to top of head.

Middle frequencies, two laughs (subconscious)

Ha, ha, ha!

Thoracic spine region from heart-lungs up to throat

heh, heh, heh the quietest laugh

Digestive organs, right and left, belly button up to diaphragm muscle

Low frequency (unconscious)

Ho, ho, ho!

Relates with belly button down to toenails and soles of feet.

Q: Tell me more about "Hee-hee."

A: Adults tend to block "Hee, hee, hee!" because it sounds childish as in, "Tee hee!" Very young Children laugh tee--hee because they are primarily head beings. Casper the Friendly Ghost, the ultimate image of the inner child, of about three years old, the very young inner child, in his several decades of comic books, would always laugh, "Tee-hee!"

Q: Any independent verification of this idea of four vertical regions of frequency in human bodies?

A: Yes, in esoteric Hinduism thru the Theosophists. David Tansley has a technical discussion and diagram of the four frequencies of the etheric body from traditional yoga in his Radionics and the Subtle Anatomy of Man (1967 first ed?) but I never found any use for this over Bertrand's approach, over ten years of looking. The four laughs as anatomy serve all the purposes of Tansley and more.

Q: What practical application for self-healing exists?

A: Bertrand suggests the most useful way to learn about them is to identify and track back, to where reactive patterns come form in the body.

For instance, if I'm a woman and I feel jealous, when my husband looks at another woman, that's reactivity. If I am curious and wish to moderate this automatic habit, where it is recorded and playing back from, within my body, can be determined by testing thru the four laughs. The basic self knows and understands the four laughs very well; so, you can use the four laughs as a language bridge for communicating with your child within.

Four laughters as measures of inner teamwork R~L

The four laughs can be combined with the magic of

NEW Energy Anatomy

right~left. The four laughs can measure how functional we are right~left in any ONE vertical region simply by measuring how strong the appropriate laugh in that region is right~left. Is the laugh on the right side equal in strength to the laugh on the left side? Is one side stronger? Which side? The priority is always going to be the weaker side: what block or obstacle is disturbing it from healthy laughing?

.v\V/v.

~ New view FIVE ~

Our gut brain is organized top and bottom

1) Our capacity for feeling and desire is located in our body above the belly button. Our capacity for willingness is located in our body below our belly button:

Feeling and desire

Willingness

dg-22 feeling-desire

The belly button is the "o" in the diagram above.

When we are born, what happy infants have is not willpower, not willfulness, not "will"—but willingness. This is what we are trying to get back to, willingness. Crosby, Stills, Nash & Young: "We have to get ourselves back to the Garden," that's "willingness" to both live with our own nature, to live and cooperate with external Nature.

When willingness dysfunctions, it transforms into: my will, willpower, willfulness, wontfulness, resistance and againstness; in NVC terms, "fight, flight, freeze."

The topic of willingness is taken up in depth in the booklet

NEW Energy Anatomy

"Willingness is the pre-requisite to all healing."

"Feeling-desire" is the frequency of the subconscious

"Willingness" and its dysfunctions have the frequency of UN-conscious:

> **subconscious**
>
> **unconscious**

dg-23 txt dg

This close-up of our gut brain, below the diaphragm muscle, is also a close-up of our capacity of self-esteem.

> **Self-esteem in feeling**
>
> **Self-esteem in willingness**

dg-24 txt dg

The frequency of laughter above the belly button is hey,

132

hey, hey! The frequency of laughter below the belly button is Ho, ho, ho!

Healthy feeling & desire
Hey, hey, hey!

Healthy willingness
Ho, ho, ho!

dg-25

v\V/v/

NEW Energy Anatomy

~ New view SIX ~

Our gut brain has four quadrants

Because our gut brain is organized both top & bottom and right & left, this permits four quadrants. Diagrammed here as if look into a mirror or down at your own body:

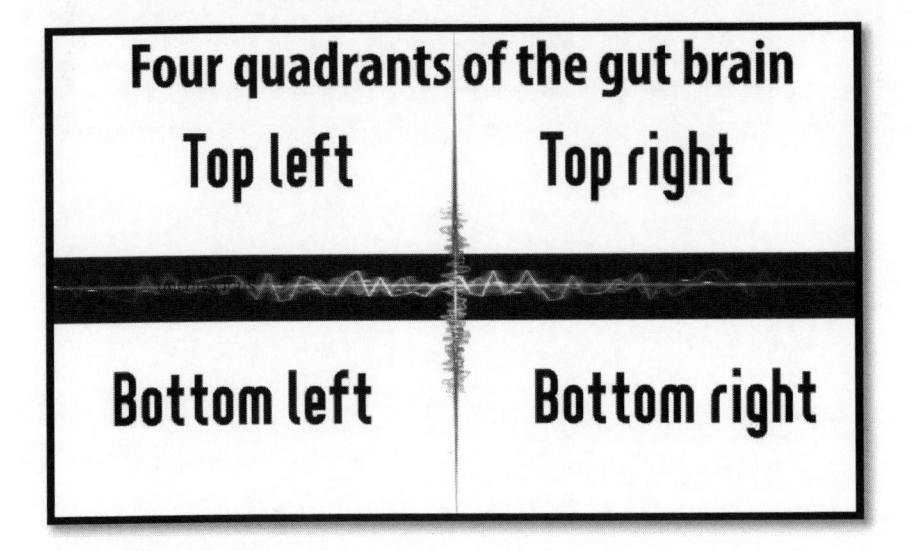

Four quadrants of the gut brain	
Top left	Top right
Bottom left	Bottom right

dg-26 txt four quads

Trying to give credit where credit is due, even tho I can't recall seeing it and even tho a Google search in 2010 for "four quadrants of TCM" has zero pages, I think buried somewhere in TCM arcana is the idea of the front of the belly having four quadrants associated with the following organs

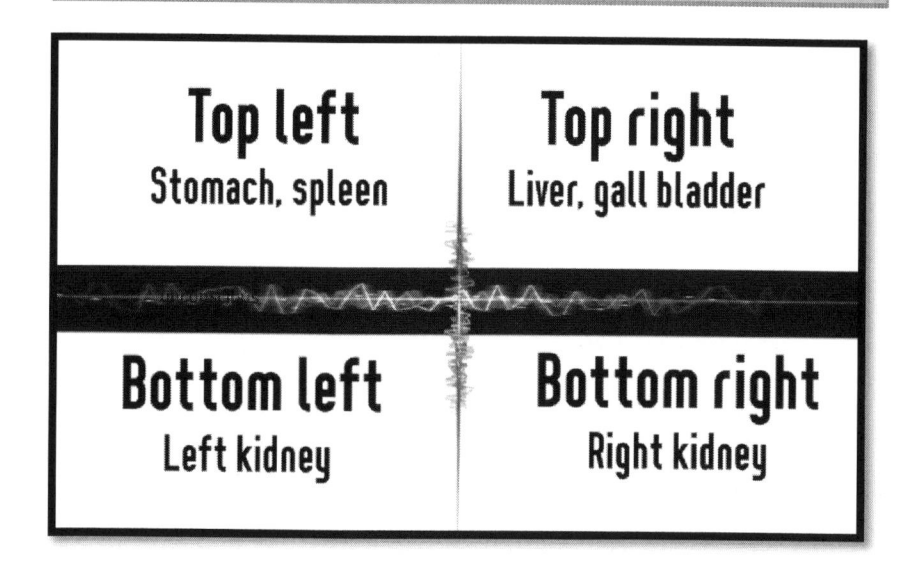

Top left Stomach, spleen	Top right Liver, gall bladder
Bottom left Left kidney	Bottom right Right kidney

dg-27 txt dg

Readers who can tie down where this exists in TCM are encouraged to contact the author to include it in the 2nd edition.

Bertrand Babinet's Inner Family in the gut

Bertrand Babinet in the early 1990s uncovered how the above quadrant-organ system from TCM(?)converges wonderfully with Virginia Satir's Family system in family therapy. Bertrand connected the characteristic expressions of family positions to the four quadrants of TCM.

NEW Energy Anatomy

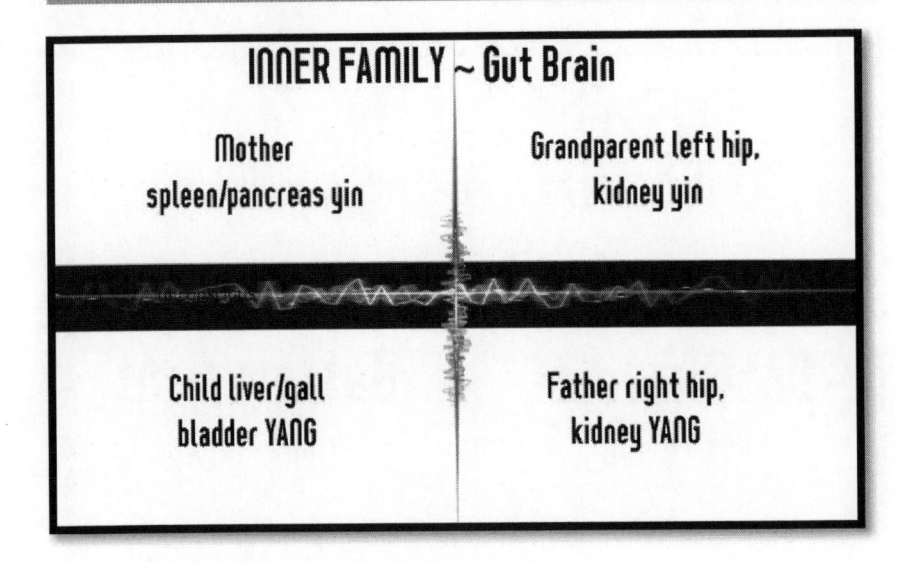

```
INNER FAMILY ~ Gut Brain

Mother                    Grandparent left hip,
spleen/pancreas yin       kidney yin

Child liver/gall          Father right hip,
bladder YANG              kidney YANG
```

The quadrant systems are taken up in full in *The Inner Court, Close-up of the Habit Body*.

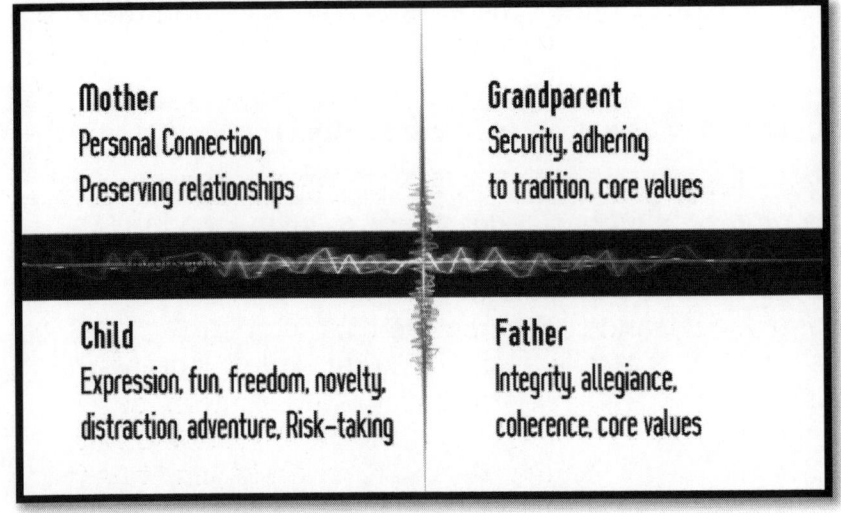

```
Mother                          Grandparent
Personal Connection,            Security, adhering
Preserving relationships        to tradition, core values

Child                           Father
Expression, fun, freedom, novelty,   Integrity, allegiance,
distraction, adventure, Risk-taking  coherence, core values
```

Because Bertrand makes four distinctions of role and reaction within the gut brain-habit body-immune system, we call this a close-up of the habit body, the inner child. The four divisions multiply the distinction possible with the term "basic self" or "inner child" alone.

Which family archetype do you play the most?

Which family relation expresses most in your own behavior? "Oh, you look like your father!" and, "You take after your mother, don't you?" Everyone has been told things like this. For purposes of self-healing, we are wise to explore our family of origin.

Inner Family members briefly characterized

Mother-Guinever	Connection, affection, rhythm, belonging, intimacy, gratitude
Child-Lancelot	Spontaniety, fun, freedom, novelty, distraction
Grandparent-Merlin	Influence with others, intellectual facility, survival of identity
Father-King Arthur	Physical integrity, strength & survival, honesty, generosity

Dg-29 InFam char txt-gif

From "Inner Family" to "Inner Court"

In 2000 the present author uncovered an alternate formulation, greatly expanding the depth possible with the Inner Family. Conveniently Arthurian Legend has four familiar archetypal figures:

Q: Which is better?

A: The inner court is slightly more useful for "what is present" with individual members. The Inner Family is slightly better for assessing and perceiving relationships,

NEW Energy Anatomy

alliances and whole-brainedness.

Many additional therapeutic insights, more angles, and more leverage, for self-healing is provided by study of The Once and Future King, etc. Where the functional and dysfunctional expressions of behaviors of all four characters are described in story form.

Inner Court members related to physical anatomy

An expanded table of the quadrants with physical organs is useful at this point:

Guinever:	Omentum, stomach, pancreas, spleen
Lancelot:	Liver, gall bladder
Merlin:	Left kidney, left hip
King Arthur:	Right kidney, right hip

Inner Court related to TCM elemental qualities:

Guinever:	Warm, sweet fertile Earth
Lancelot:	Sprouting, budding, new Wood Shoots
Merlin:	Air, metal
King Arthur:	Ice, water, fog, steam

Inner Court as William Glasser's Five Human Needs

William Glasser's *Choice Theory* (1998) is arguably his best book. In it he highlights five universal human needs:

survival, fun, freedom, belonging and power in peer relationships

These find natural homes in the four archetypes of Arthurian legend:

Guinever > belonging

Lancelot > fun, freedom

Merlin > security > security as survival of identity, meaning, purpose and status among peers

King Arthur > security as survival of physical body, ethics and purpose

The above table can be fleshed out usefully like this:

> **Mother-Guinever** Connection, affection, rhythm, belonging, intimacy, gratitude
>
> **Child-Lancelot** Spontaniety, fun, freedom, novelty, distraction
>
> **Grandparent-Merlin** Influence with others, intellectual facility, survival of identity
>
> **Father-King Arthur** Physical integrity, strength & survival, honesty, generosity

NEW Energy Anatomy

Dg-32 txt InCt needs

Notice how the five "goals" correlate with the Inner Court in a very stable fashion. We all want each of these good things. Can you think of anyone who does NOT want belonging, fun, security, power & freedom?

Yet, each of us wants these in different amounts. Each person prioritizes these five uniquely.

Glasser encourages you to prioritize your own five needs. Readers can easily assign different point values to each need and see what rises to top.

Glasser constructs such "needs profiles" and compares the profiles of business partners, potential marriage mates, parents and their teens and so on.

Guinever, Lancelot, Merlin, King Arthur are convenient to abbreviate as GLMA.

GLMA as Supporter, Promoter, Analyzer, Controller

A 1980s personality typology, whose exact origin is unknown to me, posits four archetypal roles, *Supporter, Promoter, Analyzer* and *Controller*. These offer many insights on the Inner Court:

> Guinever > emotional maturity > *Supporter*
>
> Lancelot > Enthusiasm > *Promoter*
>
> Merlin > Learning style > *Analyzer*
>
> King Arthur > Executive ability > *Controller*

The most visual model of the human psyche

20th century psychology, even including holistic innovations thru 1999, did not achieve any striking nor almost any coherent *visual* iconography I can think of. Transactional Analysis probably came closest to a visual iconography for the human psyche. Without an explicitly spiritual component, TA's iconography did not make it into the 21st century with any momentum.

The Inner Court bypasses or ignores many abstractions familiar to 20th century psychologists. The Inner Court encourages visual representations for all functional and dysfunctional psychic aspects, as much as this is possible. ALL of the following are preferred over abstractions:

Physical body posture, body image, clothing, accessories, room environment, etc.,

Images of goals and needs including color and intensity,

Emotional coloring,

Mental images and metaphors for beliefs,

Archetypal myths, roles and characters,

Images of God, Divinity and Ultimate Authority.

Each of these potential *visual* reference points can verified and validated simply by tested with any form of muscle testing. Such subjective verification works because these reference points are only valid, and need only be valid, in the domain of one person. Additional research since 2000 suggests two practitioners working together, observing the same target phenomena, do receive quite similar impressions, both by testing and by clairvoyance.

NEW Energy Anatomy

As observed in other writing, body-based models and psychologies appear to have a decided edge over abstract psychologies. The Inner Family-Court appears compatible with all body-based imagery down to anatomical detail, if useful. This is a strength.

For instance if you don't have a handy body worker who can find, access and massage your left psoas muscle, you can get at this muscle thru the body images of the Inner Court and assess if unresolved issues are making the muscle unnecessarily tight.

The rich visual characterizations of the Inner Court enhance vague conventional language, such as, "I feel good," or "I feel lousy." Such overly-broad statements sometimes provide little therapeutic direction. The poor-- or greatly improved posture and carriage in the appearance of one Inner Court member is often much more evocative of self-healing.

It may be our habit body can finally be explored by the presence--or absence--of the most simple and mundane visual detail imaginable.

Which Inner Court archetype are you most like?

Which archetype of Arthurian legend does my expression and behavior gravitate towards? Do I act more like Guinever, Lancelot, Merlin, or King Arthur?

Do you guess this will have much to do if you are right-side-dominant, left-side-dominant, top-dominant or bottom-dominant? Then you guess correctly.

For example I, Bruce, express with a personality highly colored by Guinever & Merlin on the left side in the gut and the rear of the head. If you look up both the section on positive and negative qualities of Guinever & Merlin in the Inner Court book, you get a picture of my personality expression in some depth.

Many healers and counselors have strong affinity with Guinever in the Inner Court. We want to acknowledge Guinever is the iNtuitive Feeling (NF) one in the Inner Court, the peacemakers, the nurturers, the caregivers and the forgivers. When dysfunctional, we overgive, are doormats, the co-dependent enablers of abusive partners.

Guess what else? During this entire lifetime, the great majority of my physical problems are left-sided. This is true for anyone who has primarily Guinever and/or Merlin issues. With recent uncovery of Heart Psychology thanks to Julie Motz' *Hands of Life*, we're learning my left-sided issues are also somehow connected with the left two quadrants of my heart muscle being stronger than the two right quadrants of my heart muscle. Stay tuned as we explore this.

So what's your pattern? Have you found it yet?

LEFT TOP dysfunction ~ GUINEVER – Mother

Overcharge dysfunction: Obsessed with own needs, whining. Over-identification with relationships.

Undercharge dysfunction: Feeling rejected Feeling disappointed, "doormat," taking abuse, emotional neglect, indecisive, procrastination.

RIGHT TOP dysfunction ~ LANCELOT – child

Overcharge dysfunction: Me, me, me! Look at me, daddy! Expand and scatter my own forces, succumbing to distractions

Undercharge dysfunction: withdrawn, withholding,

NEW Energy Anatomy

unexpressed anger and resentment.

LEFT BOTTOM dysfunction ~ MERLIN– grandparent:

Overcharge dysfunction: Mr. Know It All, not learning, over-identification with inheritance of traditional wisdom & possessions.

Undercharge dysfunction: Feeling abandoned, not learning.

RIGHT BOTTOM dysfunction ~ KING ARTHUR – father

Overcharge dysfunction: Bully, control freak. Over-identification with outer world power and possessions.

Undercharge dysfunction: Feeling betrayed, indecisive, procrastination

Both Guinever & Lancelot dysfunctional: over-liking, under-liking, infatuations, prejudices, unhealthy playing of roles.

Both Merlin & Arthur dysfunctional: Willfulness, wontfulness, resistance, againstness, fear, doubt, confusion, unresolved unconscious issues.

Right and left side "teams" in the solar plexus

Your left side	Your right side
Stomach pancreas spleen	Liver gall bladder

dg-R~L teams txt

This is our yin-YANG split in the body, left-right. Differences between our left and right sides are visible in our musculature, see *The Body Reveals*, 2nd ed. and in differences between left and right eyes (our eye differences also tell us about differences top and bottom in our body).

Q: Can the two sides ever be switched, YANG on the left, yin on the right?

A: I know one man who is a medical oddity; his liver is on the left, heart on the right, all the organs switched left for right. Professor doctors used him to play practical jokes on med students in college. His YANG was still on the right and yin on the left. So this is a good example of an exception proving the rule: YANG on right, yin on left.

People sometimes FEEL stronger on their left side, especially if they are left-hand-dominant. This means they are left-side dominant. This is not the same as YANG has switched sides. Check to see if they are more conscious of their needs (L) or goals (R).

Some women are stronger in their right side.

NEW Energy Anatomy

Some men are stronger in their left side.

Our relaxing, nourishing, calming, smiling energy, yin capacity is on our left side. This energy is well represented by the archetypes of Merlin and Guinever.

Our outward-turning, exuberant capacity, YANG, energy is on our right side. This energy is well-represented by the archetypes of King Arthur and Lancelot.

Which is better? Both.

YANG-dominant people--that's most of us in the industrialized West--are action-oriented and goal-oriented, the go-getters. At the solar plexus, the right side will be preferred.

YANG go-getters are prone to "YANG-banging," exhausting their YANG; leading to, yin deficiency on the left side of their bodies. This is often out-pictured in how intimate relationships can lag behind and take a back seat to striving and initiative to how they will take the world by storm.

The reverse case, left-side-dominant in the gut is just the reverse. The 'sensitive new age man' or woman often out-pictures this dominance pattern.

Because these energetic dominance patterns exist, most individuals have more right or more left-sided problems in their body

This connects with preference for either yin or YANG activity in the body and how balanced they are.

Is my b/s male or female?

Bertrand Babinet says he was often asked by pregnant mothers, "Is my baby going to be a boy or a girl?" He told us a better question to ask.

Bertand's better question is, will the newborn be more yin-dominant or YANG-dominant in the physical body?

If you have ever met a biker chick comfortable with her own female role, you will grasp one way this can play out. Your preference for polarity is not 100% consistent with your choice of gender.

Your habit body can get used to almost anything, one of its great assets.

This "overlapping" of genders and polarities possibility is a major mechanism towards androgeny, more balance between masculine and feminine roles in local culture.

Find a more discussion of these issues in *The Three Selves, Vol. 1*.

R~L sides of our bodies as younger and older

In our first view of R~L sides, we said the reality of our right side as younger and left side as older only becomes fully apparent when we know something about Lancelot and Arthur on our right side and Guinever and Merlin on our left side. That time has come.

One of the keys here is that in Arthurian legend, Guinever is twice the age of Lancelot. They are only the same age in movies and musicals for commercial reasons, for reasons of "date nite" audiences. Once it's understood that Guinever is an older woman, it's obvious both Merlin, the Grandparent in Bertrand's Inner Family system and Guinever are the wisdom-carriers of the Inner Court.

Lancelot, the child in Bertrand's system, and Arthur are the younger, more outgoing pair. This suggests we have more inspiration and determination on our right and

NEW Energy Anatomy

wisdom won from life lessons on our left, and so it is. Our left side is where our skills as diplomats live and breathe.

Further, in our left side also lives wisdom of group process and metaphysics. Lancelot is famously drawn to metaphysics but on our right side we have more youthful inspiration and aspiration than mature accomplishment.

.v\V/v.

~ New view SEVEN ~

Four quadrants of our head brain

The four quadrant pattern in our gut is duplicated in our head, but freshly arranged.

The fact of TWO quadrant sets and their geometrical facts has much to do with what we call puberty. What we call puberty is well-defined as the switching-over from gut-brain dominance in children; to, head-brain dominance in adults. This is spelled out in *The Five Puberties, A 3S journal on children.*

First let's go back to the diagram of how we are organized top and bottom, into self concept above and self-esteem below.

It should not surprise that if our lower enteric nervous system and self-esteem is organized into four quadrants, why not also the cerebral nervous system and our self-concept?

Similarly to the gut, our self-concept, in our head, is organized into four quadrants, front and back, right and left.

The c/s is turned 90 degrees from the b/s

The Inner Court down in our solar plexus is arranged on a vertical plane, on the front of our belly, so to speak, like a window with four equal square panes of glass.

The Inner Court in our head is arranged on a horizontal plane, like a chess board with only four equal squares.

NEW Energy Anatomy

One vertical, one horizontal, a difference of 90 degrees between the b/s and c/s.

The 90 degree difference between head and gut is not intended as a natural barrier. However it does explain some things! No wonder some times your right hand doesn't know what your left hand is doing! No wonder communicating with yourself and your inner child is not as automatic as we wish it was.

Quadrants of the brain:

In the standing person, the quadrants of the brain form a plane horizontal to the Earth. The Inner Court in the head, looking down on yourself from above. Top is front; bottom is rear.

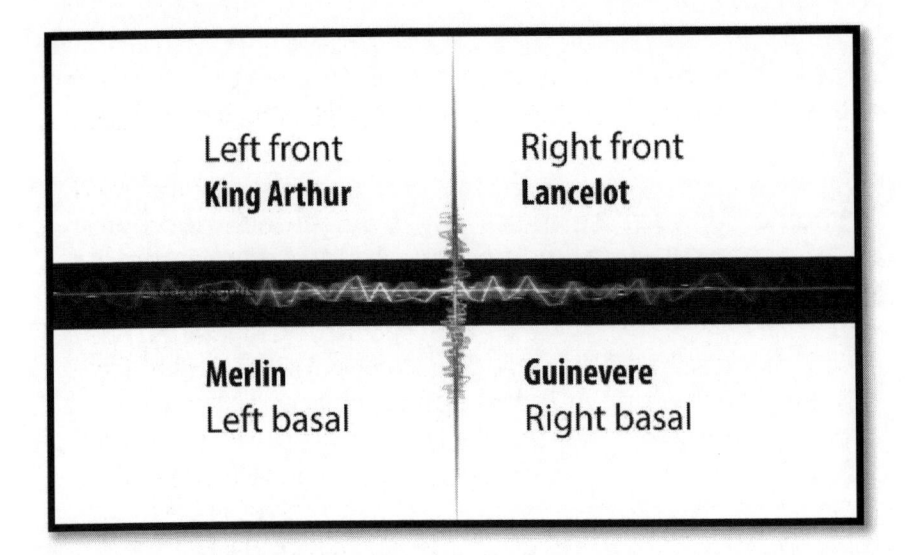

Left front **King Arthur**	Right front **Lancelot**
Merlin Left basal	**Guinevere** Right basal

Dg-34 cerebral In Ct

Merlin in the left rear brain is kin with the stereotype of the wizened green-eye-shaded accountant in the dim, rear office, counting the money and keeping the books.

If this part is strong, this is where we "make things right," where we like things "just so," our sense of completion, the part who breathes a sigh of relief when

- the project is finished,

- the numbers add it,

- the answer is found,

- the car insurance is paid up,

- the last payment on the mortgage is made.

It likes accounts settled--or to know how they will be settled. This part enjoys closing curtains, turning off unnecessary lights and straightening the crooked pictures on the wall. Here, organization, structure and more generally "form," is good for its own sake.

Myers-Briggs calls this the Judging part. The connotations of "judgmental" mislead and are emotionally inappropriate. Too many of the horror stories about MBTI gone wrong in MBTI workplace trainings have to do with just this term. This quadrant simply likes closure and absolutes. It likes things settled. So we propose "judging" be stricken from MBTI and replaced with Closure (C) as in "prefers Closure." This also dovetails with the initial for Maryann Castellanos' Cerebral dominant.

If Merlin is weak (undercharged) then these issues of closure do not interest him. things can always be straightened up and rectified tomorrow, right?

Children exercise this capacity for order in using building blocks to build up big castles.

NEW Energy Anatomy

Right rear brain: Guinever

A good modern characterization of Guinever in the right rear brain is the blissful, happy, heartfelt young female kindergarten teacher in her classroom. Even on days she teaches poorly, the kids love her!

The right rear basal part of the brain is just the opposite of the left basal. It does not view the world in terms of completions. This part cares little for closure. It is in no hurry to settle matters. Guinever views the world as it is moment to moment, taking in the world spontaneously. She's into expansion, expanding horizons. Her Kindergarten students thrive on her expansiveness and want it for themselves. She delights in spaciousness, freedom, color sound, taste and touch for their own sake. Each day is brand new to this part when happy.

This is the part of us who knocks down the wooden block castle so something new, better and less restrictive can be built.

As in right brain lit, this is the part who recognizes things by gestalts: faces, gestures, sounds, etc.

Myers-Briggs calls this the Perceiving part. We propose amending the P designation in MBTI to P for sPontaneous as being a more clear characterization.

Which is better, Closure or sPontaniety? Both.

Arthur, front left, is General George Patton

Also General Douglas Mac Arthur of WW II fame. This is our executive ability. You hear a lot about the *loss* of executive ability in brain study of autistic and ADHD kids. This ability rests primary in the left front quadrant. This is the first capacity to disappear in progressive brain deterioration. Arthur and Lancelot are the two characters of executive ability in Camelot. They are in front in terms of the healthy adult conscious self.

Lancelot, front right, is James Thurber

The front right position is the 1930s New Yorker poet, cartoonist and humorist James Thurber. Maybe also Jules Feiffer: artfulness. Thurber was much beloved for his whimsical view of life and his great tolerance and acceptance of the eccentricities of behavior in ordinary people. Thurber was considered rather eccentric himself and you can get a sense of his novel sense of humor and experimental thinking in his New Yorker cartoons.

Antoine de Saint-Exupery, the French author, journalist and pilot who wrote *The Little Prince* in 1943, one year before his death, also comes to mind. His other book, *Wind, Sand and Stars*, has the same quality in a more artful childlikeness in an adult tale.

If you know anything of Patton and Thurber/ Exupery, you will glean how diametrically opposite the two expressions are. This suggests how wide the maximum range of talents is potentially in just the front two brain quadrants. What if *both* these talents were supported, nurtured and protected in young children? That's what enlightened whole-child education tries to do.

Fifth element in the head?

Where's the fifth element in the head? If the soul has a location in the physical body, it is near the center of the brain, behind the eyes and between the ears, the tisra til, where inner sound, the sound current, is perceived.

NEW Energy Anatomy

Our human brain wakes up and develops from back to front

Very comprehensive pictures of this process as a stage development process can be gained from most Waldorf education texts pertaining to the young child. *You Are Your Child's First Teacher,* 2nd ed, by Rahima Baldwin; and, *Teaching as a Lively Art,* by Marjorie Spock, are especially recommended and available at many libraries. From birth to adulthood, the brain develops, grows, matures and "wakes up" from back to front. In the first eight years the vast majority of connections and wiring is made in the rear two quadrants. This naturally includes how you think and feel about yourself as a boy or a girl. This "me-ness" is often discussed as gender-identity,

By age eight we have probably encountered some school system. We make decisions about how difficult or easy school learning is for us, how much work it is to absorb the material and how strongly connected we are with the school system and reward culture. Call this "me-ness" self-concept and learning style.

Rear brain quadrants as J~P in MBTI

Merlin in the left rear brain quadrant pertains to what we have learned and how we have learned it, our learning styles, not only content. If the inner Merlin is nurtured, encouraged and protected from feeling nerdy and left out, healthy closure (Judging) can develop as a personal preference, confident and not too closed-minded.

The right rear quadrant likes to have fun, as in "Girls Just Want to Have Fun" and is attuned to who is making an impression on whom, who is reacting to whom and how. MBTI makes clear it's not just artsy people and actors who care about performance. Craftsmen, athletes and brain surgeons all appear to have a preference for sPontaneous. When Guinever's love of space, play, movement, art and relationship is inspired in healthy ways, she grows up with a preference for being sPontaneous in life, confident and not too scattered.

One or the other of these two is always more developed, at least 51%, leading to a preference for either closure or spontaneity.

As the rear two quadrants, in the adult conscious self, Merlin and Guinever are the more unconscious, supportive, retiring, in the background, gone but not forgotten yet often taken for granted.

The four brain quadrants in self-healing

Many aspects of how the Inner Court in the gut applies to self-healing also apply to the Inner Court in the head.

A natural progression exists in self-healing. First work on reducing excess reactivity in the gut. Later on, move to uncovering unresolved disturbances in the head. We are so "close" to our head activity, we have less objectivity on it than we do on our gut.

We are much more conscious of disturbed activity in our gut than we are of disturbed activity in our head. This may be why the Waldorf people say age 35 is the "normal" time to begin a path of personal-spiritual growing, if you have not already begun.

It may be later proven that our gut brain is more of a sub-conscious frequency (higher towards the surface of awareness) while our head brain activity is more of an unconscious frequency (lower and farther away from awareness). The amazing thing is how accessible these aspects are once you know what you are looking for!

The four brain quadrants exercise some control over the

NEW Energy Anatomy

four gut quadrants. This mechanism remains mysterious yet it may be like how the leaves high up on a tree are connected with the trunk further below.

A general principle seems to be if it has cleared in the head, it can clear in the gut. If it has NOT cleared in the head, it's more difficult to clear in the head first.

This aligns with embryology how, in the womb, the entire body "unwraps" or spirals out from the head.

For example, Guinever in the head "controls" Guinever in the gut. Disturbances in Guinever in the gut ultimately have to also be cleared in G. in the head because that is where many of them are coming from. So often if we find a gut issue, we can go up to the head and learn how that issue looks "upstairs."

The four quadrants of the body

I suppose there are many ways to get to the idea of four quadrants of the body. I got to it thru the Inner Court in the head.

The four body quadrants begin with GLMA in the gut.

G can stand for the upper left quadrant of the body, above the diaphragm muscle.

L can stand for the upper right quadrant of the body, above the diaphragm muscle.

M can stand for the lower left quadrant of the body, below the diaphragm muscle.

A can stand for the lower right quadrant of the body, below the diaphragm muscle.

So now we are talking larger, more subtle fields in the body. How to work with these in self-healing? So far one thing that seems to work well is to "target" one set, say Merlin in the head and the lower left quadrant and simply chant love into both of them. The "HU" or "Ani-Hu" work well for me.

How Inner Court in the head affects Inner Court in the gut

Strength and ability in the front half of the brain, will show up as confidence, strength and ability on the right side of the gut brain, in Lancelot and King Arthur (liver-gall bladder) and kidney YANG.

Strength and ability in the rear half of the brain, will show up as confidence, strength and ability on the left side of the gut brain, Guinever and Merlin (stomach-pancreas-spleen), kidney yin and the immune system.

Speculation on other arrangements

The arrangement of quadrants differs, head and gut, as above. This is original basic research. If you find additional patterns, please do share them. I'm a student here too.

The top lead pair, in our gut are Guinever and Lancelot.

The front lead pair in our brain are Arthur and Lancelot.

This is the same for both men and women.

What does this tell us? It signifies the differing character between the b/s and the c/s. The lead pair are not the same in both.

NEW Energy Anatomy

When we are children, before puberty, we are Lancelot and Guinever: feeling. When young children scrape their knee or are injured or even get their feelings hurt, everything stops until we get taken care of.

Arthur and Merlin are active in the young child but primarily in dreamlike expressions, if at all.

At puberty the c/s is going to come into its own. The topic of "The reversal of learning style at puberty," is taken up in detail in this author's, *The Five Puberties, Temperament & Typology, a 3S Journal*.

Nature knows this is going to happen. If Lancelot and Guinever were also the two front brain quadrants, we'd have no incentive and maybe no possibility to grow up and mature. We would be powerfully persuaded to remain children. Instead nature arranges things so only one of our childhood allies Lancelot is up front in the brain.

The topic of cross-synergy in the Inner Court, augmenting the four quadrant system, is taken up in *The Inner Court, Close-up of the Habit Body*.

RIGHT~left converged with Inner Court

It turns out the Inner Court has another great practical use for addressing physical concerns if we explore further in how we are organized right-left AND organized in the Inner Court.

Foot issues are the best example to learn on. If your physical left foot hurts, and after you have cleared all the misunderstandings related to how you arrange things to get your own physical, emotional and sexual needs met, what do you do if your left foot still pains you?

Check the left foot of Inner Court members on your RIGHT side in your head.

It's very common in my experience that unresolved problems in our physical left foot often track back to our RIGHT side, but to the LEFT foot of Inner Court members in the right side of our head.

Many readers will grasp this is a kind of crossing over, and "crossing the midline" but also "turned ninety degrees" as well.

Same with shoulder issues: check the Inner Court members on the opposite side of the body.

Same with unresolved tooth issues: check the Inner Court members on the opposite side of the body.

.v\V/v.

NEW Energy Anatomy

~ New view EIGHT ~

Back of our head: willingness to heal our own past

Our eighth etheric center is in the back of our head. Conventional anatomy and psychology term this the "reptile brain." This not one physical structure alone; rather, it includes the brain stem and as many other nearby structures as you are on good terms with.

I never liked the term "reptile brain" so it took me a long time to first understand and live into the reptile aspects; and then, to identify more artful imagery. A full explication of the reptile aspects of our rear brain is beyond our scope here. See Maryann Castellanos' work on this.

Axis of function in the back of the head

The back of the head functions on an axis between; on one hand:

A palace of light, a castle of light, a feeling of safety and easy permeability thruout our entire inner community. The whole castle in Sleeping Beauty, that fell asleep, when she fell asleep, the castle is altogether wakened back into normal

dg-demolished city

healthy function.

On the other hand:

dg-35 healthy walled city

A completely demolished city. Where a walled city used to be, now there is not one stone standing upon another (i.e. Crusades, Hiroshima, etc)Feelings of self-dissolution and homelessness.

In the healthy walled city

All needed incoming impressions can "enter into town" easily and all outgoing messages to 'surrounding communities' go out easily and unimpeded, even to the furthest reaches of the kingdom, the most hinter lands.

This is not "anything goes" or an" open door policy." Trained guardians monitor the inflow and outflow of traffic, alert to any and all safety issues and violations. This is an orderly processes of growth and regulation.

NEW Energy Anatomy

Overcharge and undercharge in back of the head

As with all other meridians, organs and glands, dysfunction occurs on an axis of, one pole undercharged, one pole overcharged. See this spelled out and applied to organs and meridians in Meridian Metaphors, Psychology of the Meridians and Major Organs.

The overcharged polarity of dysfunction in the reptile brain is a walled city shut up tight, a walled city under siege, as in the times of the Crusades. No one can get in and no one can get out either. Fear, anxiety and stagnation rule.

The undercharged pole is a less than complete city with less than complete defenses and boundaries. In a completely demolished city, where walls and structures used to be, now there is not one stone standing upon another. Feelings of self-dissolution and homelessness occur.

These conditions can easily be assessed with muscle testing.

Below the walled city, the foundations

To complete the topic of our reptile brain as a walled city, our atlas, axis and vertebrae are metaphorically the "foundations" of the city and have shown up thru the metaphor of "foundations" to be checked in two clients.

.v\V/v.

~ New view NINE ~

Our hip girdle as a Ring of Loving

Hip and neck problems as energetic instability

A promising new direction exist for unraveling hip and neck physical and energetic issues.

Let's look at the "circle" of our hips; likewise, the circle of our neck.

Chiropractors often work to increase the stability of our hips and neck.

Both neck and hips appear to rest upon some common vulnerabilities. Both neck and hips apper to have similar vulnerabilities re "stability."

Speaking metaphorically, both neck and hips can be likened to a Ring of Loving. Each Ring has four links. Each link needs to be strong because a chain or a ring of chin links, is only as strong as its weakest link.

The four links come from the four possible categories of human issues mentioned in Genesis 1:1: self, other people, the world, God.

I learned about the four issues in Genesis from Bertrand Babinet. The best way to think about these is as a "filter," a way of viewing and discerning activity and content in our unconscious. This filter makes visible content that is otherwise invisible; that's its great gift.

I've used this filter to gain insight into where I am stable

NEW Energy Anatomy

and unstable in my own life. Stability is possible and desirable in all four of these dimensions.

"Self" is the first link in neck stability. "Self" in the human experience includes and starts with your physical body--self care.

Some readers may know neck pain frequently tracks back to osteoporosis; specifically, lack of adequate and sufficient magnesium in the vertebra. If this applies to you, your self care here needs attention.

Attending to this will strengthen your 'self" link in your Ring of Loving and result in more neck stability (less pain).

Calcium is soft, like chalk; it only gives our bones their shape. Magnesium gives bones their hardness and sharp definition, as in tooth enamel. The nerves to our neck, arms and hands all thread thru small openings in our neck vertebrae. When we lack magnesium, the neck vertebrae appear "fuzzy." Tingling in the arms and hands is a frequent symptom. Stress reduces Mg and vertebra need Mg to regain optimal definition, helping the nerves in their path thru the neck.

Carpel tunnel syndrome in the wrist, nine times out of ten, is this same osteoporosis, lack of magnesium.

Q: What can I do?

A: Take additional magnesium oxide (cheaper) or orotate (more expensive) both before bed and upon awakening. Intersperse with multi minerals. Buy five different brands and rotate them because your body gets bored taking the same thing daily. Q: What else can I do?

A: Get 20% solution of liquid hydrochloric acid from High Valley Chemical in Utah, some wonderful Mormon folks.

Call them. Dilute it way down to just barely drinkable. Get some powered and/or liquid cal-mag or coral calcium. Take a half teaspoon of powder and a half teaspoon of good-tasting liquid mins and wash it down with a few swigs of very dilute HCl.

If you are low on minerals, this will tend to give you a small lift in energy right away!

Q: When do I take this?

A: Your body only lays down new bone matter while you are asleep. Take Mg especially right before bed.

Q: Can this improve bone density in my hips and overall?

A: Very much so.

Back to the hips. For many years, I went to my friendly neighborhood chiropractor, each time to correct a twist in my hips. The same dysfunctional twist always came back. When I started locating, identifying and clearing the four issues mentioned in Genesis Chapter one, my trips to the chiropractor ended.

Four issues in more modern terms

In more modern language these four issues are:

Self ~ Issues with our own self, inner child, health

Others ~ Issues with husband-wife, son-daughter, brother-sister, your immediate support system. Then, other people you know.

World ~ Other people you do not know, abundance, success and prosperity, service to others you don't know.

NEW Energy Anatomy

God ~ Issues with Authority. Father. Bosses. How we connect with our own Divinity. Unlearning God as Stern Father of the Old Testament. Relearning God as Nurturing Parent of the New Testament.

Self, Others, World, God can be abbreviated as SOWD.

Q: So how do I determine where my weakest links are?

A: There is no one right way. The only way we know fro SURE does NOT work is not to try at all. You CAN do this yourself and I encourage it. If you can go thru the categories of creativity and feel how you are doing in each, I celebrate that. If you need a scale, I recommend a scale of one-to-ten (1-10).

If you get stuck, give me a call.

Using this "map" I was able to chunk down my hip instability, solve various pieces and gradually tramp my way out of going to chiropractor for good, at least for hip instability!

Four spheres of relationship in the 3D world

The four links in a Ring of Loving can also be imagined as concentric spheres of color.

Issues with your self

The smallest sphere is issues you have with your own basic self, your inner child, your habit body, and your physical health. In short, "inner cooperation." You could have undercharge or overcharge here: too few or too much self-care, too few or two many creature comforts.

Issues with other people. Today we would say, "family" or "your personal social support system," "other people you know" in this sense.

The next largest color sphere is your relationship with other people you know. Unresolved issues with Mother, Father; wife, husband; sisters, brothers, family, friends, lovers, other people you know. Example: the "tribe" you grew up with, the tribe you have around you now.

Issues with the world

The next largest color sphere is your relationship with the rest of the 3D world: Unresolved issues with job, money, career, and service. Many issues with abundance, prosperity and riches can be found here. Example: the world owes me a living! Example: Dishonoring the Earth, its resources or environment by mining or exploiting Earth's riches in past times solely for greed.

Issues with God (how I connect with my own Divinity)

The next largest color sphere is your relationship with how you connect with your own divinity. If you have no spiritual practice whatsoever, this can be about your resentment or even anger at outer authority: bosses, father figures, the Establishment. Ultimately these issues are about how you are getting along with or not getting along with, your own soul, your own loving.

There is no one judging my performance outside of my own Divinity. Any judgment I make of myself comes from error, misuse of my inability to have compassion, understanding and forgiveness.

My disowned personal power is easily projected out onto figures and institutions. Examples: blaming God, projecting anger, hurt, blame onto God: "Why do bad things happen to good people? Why me?" How we feel about behaving like the Prodigal Son/Daughter.

Back to the hips as a Ring of Loving

NEW Energy Anatomy

"Hip instability" can indeed be broken down, "chunked down," into four issues, each of which can be measured and addressed one at a time.

One of the four categories of issues will show up as the highest priority to address in testing.

Also useful to check the depth of the issue and the willingness to heal in this issue-area.

Q: What if I don't know which area my instability is in?

A: You DON'T have to know; you only have to ask! Your rational self is unlikely to know the category of your issue. This four-fold division works best on UNCONSCIOUS issues. That's why it's so useful.

Practice testing and checking and you will learn how easy unconscious issues are to get at. This four-fold breakdown is the first distinction I go after when I come across an unconscious issue in myself or with a patron. These are highly conditioned; you simply need better questions (tools) to learn what's going on.

As we unpack these and add language, we begin to see how we are doing in these four areas of life.

Each of us wants to be responsible for allowing, promoting and creating healthy choices in each of these categories

My Ring of Loving, where is it weak?

The four categories of human issues can be conceived of as a Ring of Loving. The more solid, whole and strong this Ring is, the brighter the Light of our psyche is.

Q: Why is this a Ring and not a line?

A: Because loving your self, loving your own inner child is similar in frequency to loving your own Divinity. Loving yourself in the lower frequency is similar to loving yourself in the higher frequencies. You may recall hearing the two are not separate!

So all four of these make a convenient Ring of Loving. You won't be surprised to hear that everyone, me included, is stronger in some categories and weaker in others. If you conceive of this as a ring, you can imagine the possibility of a weak link that could benefit from more of your attention.

A while back now, the weak links in my own Ring of Loving were two, Other people and the World. I'm happy to say the operation to upgrade all links to excellence was a success and the journey was altogether lovely. Working with my mentors in Medical Intuition to get to the inner barriers that were blocking me was well worth, my time, effort and expense. I could feel the broken links and my willingness to heal was high. How long did it take? About five years. Yours might not take that long.

Anyone who can self-test can begin identifying where your weakest link is in your Ring of Loving and begin a healing process.

You can also call me a gift session where I do just this in terms of your Success Profile reading. We find the lowest number, the weakest link; and, I assist you to raise it using my large tool box of Tools That Heal, see ToolsThatHeal.com.

The four issues can also be...

NEW Energy Anatomy

Lining up for success

RIGHT~*left* in the body

To be optimally successful in the Outer Game of Success, we have to play the Inner Game of Success well because the Outer is a reflection of the Inner.

We want to be "firing on all cylinders" right and left.

If we combine two views, R~L integration with the four apanas of ho ho, hey hey, ha ha, hee hee, we get another Tool That Heals, for those looking for such tools.

Converging these two tools suggests looking at our R~L cooperation and teamwork, up and down in the body:

Hee ~ Are my two brain hemispheres synchronizing? ___/10

Ha ~ Are my two lungs lifting me as wings of my heart, beating to the rhythm of love? ___/10

Hey ~ Are R~L digestive organs affectionate, feeling good about each other? ___/10

Ho ~ Are my two kidneys hugging in an embrace focused on what I am passionate about? ___/10

Ho ~ Are hips and legs working as a team to get to the same goal? ___/10

If you find a number you wish to raise up, there are lots of things to try; including, do my kidneys feel SAFE to work together as a loving team?

HealingToolbox.org

Are my lungs WILLING to work together as a loving team?

$$\backslash v \backslash V / v /$$

NEW Energy Anatomy

Intro to the Three Selves
The nature of human nature
Simply the clearest model of the whole person

Three Selves & the Inner Court

20th century culture gave us many gifts, most of them material in nature. Two "soft" gifts, closely related to each other, were missing; and have become, conspicuous by their absence.

20th century mainstream, legacy culture conspicuously LACKED a K-12 education leading students into thinking for themselves about how to find and follow their own unique dreams into adulthood.

The other gift CONSPICUOUSLY MISSING was a psychology of mental-emotional health; including:

- A picture of the healthy nature of human nature, high school students could understand, appreciate and become excited about lifelong mental-emotional wellness,

- A "toolbox" of methods, techniques people can use when we go off track a healthy mental-emotional track and wish to come back into balance.

This is where the Three Selves comes in. It's a model of the whole human psyche both comprehensive and simple. It can coherently model any human behavior or phenomena you can throw at it so habits can be tracked and re-directed as desired. I know of no other model of the psyche with this range of applicability. I wish more existed!

The greatest utility of the 3S is not explaining alien abduction, human combustion and multiple personaliites; tho it can do this. Rather, its greatest use is in K-college education, healing and wellness, at all levels, wherever a coherent vision of healthy, functional human nature, is needed.

Aspects of the 3S are simple enuf to be shared with and understood by five year olds. High school seniors, college freshman and sophomores can grasp the entire model and how it addresses the logic of karma.

If we take a healthy internal picture of the nature of human nature, as young adults, it becomes a gift that keeps on giving thruout life.

The 3S is the completely Westernized version of the Hawaiian wisdom of Huna-Kahuna-Ho'oponopono. Before 1950, the traditional and only way to learn about the 3S was to study and acquire a working knowledge of the Hawaiian language. This is what students of Ho'oponopono aspire to.

Max Freedom Long began the process of distilling the wisdom of indigenous Hawaiian shamen into English concepts and language. He did this complete with errors and shortcomings. John-Roger in the 1970s and 1980s encouraged his students to read *The Secret Science at Work*, and clarified many of the concepts from his own inner world experiences, high school teaching and psychology jobs.

The only comprehensive textbook on the westernized Three Selves so far attempted is *You Have Three Selves; Simply the clearest model of the whole person* vols. 1&2 available HERE: http://www.amazon.com/Bruce-Dickson-MSS/e/B007SNVG46

The 3S appears to be the best candidate for a "big tent" for psychology within which the greatest number of

NEW Energy Anatomy

approaches to the psyche can find common ground and gain from each other.

Q: How can the 3S be navigated when virtually all of it is invisible, except for outer behavior?

A: Self-muscle testing of any kind, including dowsing, can be used to explore, acknowledge, clarify, identify issues into conventional mental-emotional language.

Q: How do I know what to test for or ask?

A: You don't have to know. Maryann Castellanos says, "You don't have to know; you only have to ask."

.v\V/v.

To Learn More

Handy map of Creation, Spiritual Geography PACME, short version

If we define "psyche" as all the conditioned aspects of the human being, including the physical body; then in this sense, "psyche" is identical to "personality" as long as the body is considered part of both.

A shorthand map of Creation is useful as another way to locate conditioned aspects of our psyche, calling for our attention.

Our psyche not only has three levels of creativity, waking, dreaming and sleeping; it has five levels of frequency that reflect, in microcosm the macrocosm of God's manifested body. So a map can be useful to navigate.

Q: I don't need any map. I know who I am and what I am.

A: That's the confidence of the conscious self, very needed to get anything done here in 3D. Still, our personality is active on five levels. The only one of our five bodies NOT functioning 24 hours a day is our conscious rational mind.

We aren't taught much even about this part of our psyche is school. Did you know your rational mind can be either thinking or feeling dominant? Well, that's another topic. See The Three Selves, Vol. 1.

Here's the thumbnail view of Spiritual Geography from low frequency to high as John-Roger has given it many, many times:

NEW Energy Anatomy

P literally physical material, chemicals, minerals

A (originally "astral"), imaginal, imagination and wish realm

C emotional (originally "causal" as in "causes of our karma")

M mental, beliefs, judgments, evaluation of all kinds

E unconscious, memories, habits behaviors (originally "etheric")

Thumbnail view from high frequency to low; and, given the above definitions: UMEIP:

Spiritual Geography from low frequency to high

P ~ physical can also be called => Cellular (C)

A ~ astral can also be called => Imaginal (I)

C ~ causal can also be called => Emotional (E)

M ~ mental

E ~ etheric can also be called => Unconscious (U)

Below the Cosmic Mirror is Creation, the realms of the Mother-God, comprised of five levels of conditioned energy. Starting on the bottom . . .

PACME detail ~ low frequency to high frequency

In this model, at the top of conditioned Creation is a "Cosmic Mirror" a phrase used by both Twitchell and John-Roger. Creation below the Cosmic mirror is the domain of the Mother-God. Starting from the Cosmic Mirror, going down, the lower one goes, conditioning factors increase in number and variety.

In schematic form, Creation can be pictured as striated levels of a "density column" of liquids of varied densities, self-arranging themselves in a clear glass column, in horizontal bands, according to the characteristic specific gravity of each liquid. In poetic form, we have a 100-piece orchestra making beautiful music, as a cooperative and collaborative team effort, employing a wide range of frequencies, sometimes in harmony, sometimes in dissonance, according to the musical score of the Composer.

Physical (P) or Cellular (C)

dg-liquids column

Cellular/physical, chemicals and minerals only, the chemical corpse of the human being. Perhaps surprisingly, the home of metabolic activity is not physical but in the lower etheric because metabolism is rhythmic. Nothing is technically alive if we consider only the physical. The physical is only things, only matter, material building blocks. Rocks. Not even what we call "plant life" is wholly physical. Only the dead liquids and fiber of plants are wholly physical. The truly living elements of rocks and plants have their home above the physical; true for animals and humans as well.

(e) lower etheric

This is not a part of the model as given by John-Roger but very much a part of Theosophical and Anthroposophical models. Lower etheric realm. This is the realm of vitality, Chi, and Prana. Acupuncture meridians, health aura and all phenomena related to them are here. Life energy at this level animates the visible physical "corpse" of living beings. The lower etheric is also home to diverse categories of nature spirits, fairies and devas.

Astral (A) or Imaginal (I)

The original Theosophical term was "astral realm." Astral literally means starry. Early clairvoyants were very impressed with the sparkly and colorful quality of the human aura and the appearance of disincarnate beings living on this level, who appear sparkly and colorful. The astral realm is the realm of reactivity, conflict, imagination and ambition. The imaginal realm is also home to many polarities; including, the polarity of "liking and disliking" (Rudolf Steiner 1919). It is the home of the "monkey mind," a common term for excess mental reactivity. It's the home of the animal senses; therefore in people, "fleeting feelings" and "animal passions." It's the homes of one of the energetic "blueprints" of individual human bodies, in their optimal form, shape and structure. It's also populated by Pan, devas, nature spirits, UFOs, aliens; as well as, "Star Trek" and

"Federation of Planets" activity, according to UFO experts.

Emotional (E) (antiquated: Causal realm)

Emotional realm – No longer "fleeting" but "deep emotion;" hence: emotional attachment. Emotional love. Hatred. Theosophists called this the "causal realm" because attachment was seen as the cause of our karma. Theosophy claims this realm is approximately ten times stronger than any other realm in Creation at this time. This unfamiliar idea appears abundantly borne out by observation over time: emotions have more kinetic energy than any other realm at this time in evolution.

Mental realm

Mental realm – Form and structure. Beliefs. Mentalizing. Our inner Analyzer. Our inner Critic. Judgment. Evaluations. Allegiances.

Etheric (E) or Unconscious (U) or Mythological (M)

This is the Upper etheric realm, the mythological level, home of all archetypes; including and especially, the divine feminine archetype(s); including, the endlessly fertile "Womb of Creation." On the masculine side, this is also the home of the empty void of Zen. This is the home of Mystery, famously characterized as "neither this nor that." This is the home of Goethe's "Ur concepts," Jung's archetypes and even superheroes in their function as caricatures of self-realization. It's also the home of unconscious memories, habits and behaviors.

It is the upper etheric realm that is the energetic "glue" holding the whole of Creation together, both in all of Creation, and in each individual person, each individual

NEW Energy Anatomy

cell and on upwards in larger and larger spheres of identity. The archetypal visual for this is the sphere.

If all the realms here are pictured as bands of liquid, of progressively greater density; then, the Upper Etheric is analogous to the containing glass, holding all of them, making the arrangement coherent, visible, united.

The Upper Etheric realm spans all of PACME, weaving all disparate aspects, different densities together into One Whole. The Etheric has rightly been called the "Web of Life" as it gives sentient beings the sense of being one whole rather than disconnected parts. The upper etheric is the home of the "I am" (comment from Michael Hayes).

PACME can also be concentric circles

It is also possible to arrange the scheme above into concentric circles. In this representation, higher frequency, the more introverted realms are more inner. Going outwards we encounter the more extraverted, external realms and outer expressions; all of these are towards the periphery of the concentric circles. If this reminds you of a living cell, you are on to something.

What's above Creation?

The PACME model includes incomplete lore about how the home of our immortal eternal soul is above PACME, above Creation, in what can be called Soul and Above. This region is much less amenable to mapping, charting or diagramming. Creation and Soul and Above contrast and complement each other as the two poles of a car battery (John-Roger) and is related to the polarity of feminine and masculine in ways not yet clear.

The comment of one unknown author, on the difference between Creation and Soul and Above, in paraphrase, is, in Creation (PACME), sound and light are two distinct things. In Soul and Above, sound and light are one thing. End of spiritual geography diagram.

Maybe you see the entire psyche more clearly than this map, so your comments are very welcome!

Our soul is outside of all the conditioned aspects of our psyche. Soul is choice. Soul is unconditioned.

How the soul is in the psyche but not of the psyche is a simple idea—but we have too little language in the West even to understand this simple idea.

The following short version of spiritual geography follows what is given in the many Light and Sound groups and which can be found in their literature of the last 150 years.

Q: Are there no other spiritual geographies?

A: Indeed, I have come across seven or more attempts. Thinking about this was quite active in the West after 1880 when Theosophy, from Hinduism, introduced to the West, the idea of dividing spiritual realms into levels of frequency.

If you set all the various spiritual geographies side by side, what you find is all of them are variations on a more complete and coherent version found in Light & Sound groups. Consequently the PACME or CIEMU version is the only one promoted with any vigor today that I know of. If you know of a better one, I'd be happy to hear about it.

Q: So what. What's it good for?

NEW Energy Anatomy

Our Many Selves

CIEMU suggests each of us has lots of "me's" we are accountable who we don't even know about yet.

Q: Wait, I don't like this idea of "many different me's inside."

A: *Our Many Selves* is a reality we all face sooner or later in our personal-spiritual growing. *Our Many Selves* is the name of a famous 1971 book by Elizabeth O'Connor assisting readers to explore the "fractured self" and to celebrate our diverse inner expressions. The Amazon reader reviews of Our Many Selves are quite illuminating.

Our Many Selves was herald's trumpet call to those relative few in the early 1970s who wished to escape the straight jacket of the 18th and 19th century notion that "each person is an island unto themselves." 1970s pop culture remembers, "No man is an island," from John Donne's poem. Material-scientific mainstream 20th century culture still promotes: "every man is an island." Individual isolation is a powerful handmaiden to consumerism, invoked to explain why everyone needs an isolated single family dwelling, everyone needs a car, 2.5 children, a flat screen TV—you get the idea?

.v\V/v.

Check willingness to heal FIRST for practitioners

One of the best discoveries to come out of 1:1 sessions with clients has been learning to check the client's willingness to heal--explicitly.

Only as the inner child is at least somewhat willing and open, can disturbed parts and old habits be balanced.

This follows the wisdom:

Willingness to heal is the pre-requisite for all healing -- Bertrand Babinet (AccessNaturalHealth.com; Babinetics.com)

One practitioner's dilemma

The biggest muddles I get into with healing myself and clients is mistaking, "Yes, I want to work on my issue," with high willingness to heal. Sessions begun on issues where the willingness to heal in the inner child proves to be low, meander around aimlessly. Even if I do wonderful energetic work, often the client feels "nothing happened." Same for when I work on myself and can't determine what my basic self has willingness to heal on.

Now my goal is in every session to ascertain, by measuring on a scale of 1-10, if the inner child is aligned with healing the disturbance I have in mind.

We waste a lot of time in self-healing when we forget self-healing requires the cooperation and alignment of the basic self with the stated goal of the conscious self.

NEW Energy Anatomy

How I used to do sessions

In the old days with patrons, I simply asked them, "What do you want to work on?" I asked this because the more they can narrow their "energetic target" the better the session goes. Occasionally sessions became problematic; no matter how hard or well I worked, there was little energetic shift for the client. If I dug deeper, I got better results from my point of view but client's only said, "Eh, I don't feel much." So even if I did wonderful energetic work, often the patron felt "nothing happened."

These problematic situations ended when I began assessing the client's willingness to heal on their target issue FIRST.

Case study: How I do sessions now

A client comes to me and says, "Bruce I want to work on losing weight. I've tried everything. Why am I so heavy?"

I say, "Great! That's a clear target; you know what you want. Let's check with your inner child and learn her willingness to heal on your goal."

I check with K-testing and her willingness to heal in the inner child is only 2/10.

So I tell the client, "You are of two minds. Your conscious self wants one thing but your inner child has something else in mind."

So we talk. I don't want to work until her conscious self and inner child BOTH have agreement on what to heal. I need them to be a team, working together on one goal, the same goal.

Either we find an approach to the target they both want;

or, we explore what is bothering the inner child and make that the priority.

In the second case, shifting to what the inner child wants to clear, we hear the inner child is carrying the extra weight as part of a personal protection routine.

I ask her inner child, "What is your willingness to reducing unconscious protection routines?" The inner child has 9/10 willingness to heal the issue of reducing protection patterns. The client takes great strides forward in the session because now the c/s and inner child are on the same page; they both want the same thing resolved.

Then what happens when we work now? The client STRIDES forward in the session because the c/s and inner child are on the same page; they both want the same thing resolved; they both have the same target.

The fact is, unless high willingness to heal is present, five out of ten, 5/10, or higher, the inner child is not ready to move energy towards wellness--no matter what the conscious self wants.

Clients return for repeat business with practitioners based on their perception of movement and results. Their willingness to heal has as much or more to do with how much movement takes places in a session as the skill of the practitioner. In other words, if you are ready to heal, strongly motivated to move energy, almost anyone can assist you.

Find the FAQs and how to measure willingness to heal on yourself and others can be found in a booklet, Check Willingness to Heal First! Available from Self-Healer Press.

.v\V/v.

When coaching does not work: check depth of issue

Coaches and clients sometimes come into conflict when both coach and client agree behavior X needs to change or get done, for the highest good of everyone involved. Then if the client is still unable to change or do X, X does not get done; then, coach and client can come into conflict.

From a self-healing point of view, this simply means the client is dealing with an underlying deeper issue, usually one they know nothing about.

As in most coaching work I do, I go for clearing the block first. Behavior X will change easily or on its own if I can arrange things so the client releases their inner barriers and attachments to dysfunction.

Mental age or developmental age as reference point for sub- and unconscious parts

The hardest thing we ever have to do is to grow up ~ John Bradshaw

Several aspects of mental age have proven useful to me and clients for purposes of self-healing. Here they are in no very coherent form. Readers who can revise this into greater coherency are invited to do so and send it in for the second edition.

.v\V/v.

How to make your aura brighter

NOW with the above language at our fingertips, we can probably make some a beginning at defining energetic strength.

Energetic strength is defined pretty well as how Coherent, Integrated and Aligned (CIA) you are internally.

HOW are you organized internally, in a rudimentary way, is suggested by the nine views.

Increased CIA will always allow and create a brighter aura; this will in tern allow, create and promote more outer success. This is Success from the Inside Out.

More precise language is also at hand. Maryann Castellanos (HealthyEnergetics.net) says energetic strength is primarily how integrated the basic self and conscious self are, how integrated our head brain and gut brain are, how integrated we top to bottom.

This is a topic she and I have touched on from time to time since 2005. Here's our original correspondence:

BD: Which is more relevant to strength, organ synergy; or, enteric-cerebral synergy?

MC: Strength is in part a measure of how integrated and communicative organs are with each other. The more healthy links between organs, as in Body Talk, the more strength.

However, strength is more an enteric-cerebral thing first, primarily a measure of how integrated and communicative the enteric bottom and cerebral top are with each other. Then organ communication is within that larger potential.

NEW Energy Anatomy

Maryann has been directly viewing bodies and cells clairvoyantly for 30 years, noticing what makes them stronger or weaker. While Bruce has sight into the body and can communicate with cells, he does not yet see as clearly as Maryann.

Energetic strength

Energetic strength is the goal of Huna, kahunas and Ho'oponopono. Huna and its more Western version, The Three Selves, is a "map" of the entire human psyche modeled as three living beings:

High self handles your highest frequencies,

Middle self or conscious self, handles talking and day to day decisions, a middle frequency,

Low self or basic self, or inner child, handles metabolism, digestion, habits patterns and our lowest frequencies.

While about 20 books describe and discuss Kahuna by various authors, so far the only general textbook for Western practitioners known to me is *You Have Three Selves, Vols 1 & 2.*

Our concept of sin must be changed...and made to rest on one test alone: Does the act cause an individual to be cut off by his low self from the high self? --*Gestalt and the Wisdom of The Kahunas*, p. 73, Bethal Phaigh

The less connected we are as middle selves--the yak-yak mind--from either our inner child or high self, the less whole, the less fully human we become.

"Sin is self-made law, not gods law," is another common Huna idea. Sin in this sense is what reduces energetic strength. Consequently ANYTHING that reduces feelings of sin, guilt, regret and shame increases energetic strength.

Q: Boy, I bet this has a lot to do with how easy it is to manifest success in the outer 3D world!

A: You'd be correct there. Energetic strength is a key element of the Inner Game of Business, no matter what your biz. Your business mirrors who you are, your strength and weaknesses. The more green, holistic or spiritually inclined your biz is, the stronger your biz mirrors you. Building up your own energetic strength is an indirect yet practical way to strengthen your business. Find a full discussion of this in Success 101, Winning at the Inner and Outer Games of Business.

Optimal energetic strength is possibly well-described as high measures on all ten aspects of energetic anatomy. Improvement in any one of these measures tends to increase overall energetic strength; tho, this is not always perceptible consciously.

Q: Okay! Now I'm ready for a brighter aura! All I have to do is eliminate my north-south conflicts! Oh boy, I'm ready!

A: Hmm, maybe.

The end game of New Energetic Anatomy is increasing your energetic strength. Making your aura brighter is another way of talking about increasing energetic strength and a stronger immune system.

Just as you might imagine, making your aura brighter means making it brighter top and bottom, right and left and front and back. That's this book in a nutshell.

Maryann's thinking here is this, the determining factor for increasing energetic strength—and making your aura brighter—is how integrated your two nervous systems

NEW Energy Anatomy

are, that would be your enteric and cerebral nervous systems. The more integrated and harmonious your two nervous systems are, the more collected your full psyche is; and therefore, the brighter your aura.

The topics here, a couple from Maryann, some related to Bertrand Babinet's early work, and the rest from my own self-healing process, were developed to understand, "What are the primary causative factors of energetic strength?" which can be pictured, metaphorically at least, as a brighter aura.

"Brighter aura" is perhaps most useful as a metaphor for increased personal integration and inner harmony.

Increasing inner harmony can be understood as reducing inner barriers and inner conflicts, on all levels, mostly sub- and unconscious. This intention comes many if not the majority of energetic health modalities that aim to reduce energetic disturbances, if possible before they manifest physically.

Improvements in any of these energetic measures are likely to make your aura brighter. More usefully, improvement to any of these topics will permit you to feel better, more complete, more whole, more integrated and resilient to life.

The game here is really not "to make your aura brighter." Rather the game here is use NEW Energetic Anatomy to identify and locate disturbances you can now address and clear up, reducing inner barriers and conflicts to your own personal goals.

Need tools to address an imbalance you found? Need a toolbox? HealingCoach.org is that.

Stuck on an issue? If you get stuck, give me a call.

$$.v\backslash V/v.$$

Make your cells brighter

If your cells are brighter, your aura will definitely be brighter.

We make our cells brighter by arranging our diet and lifestyle to reduce nutritional toxins and maximize nutritional benefits. The closer extra and intracellular conditions are to optimal, the more Light can flow thru your cells, making them brighter.

Bu wait! There's more! Diet and nutrition improvements only reduce physical obstacles to our cells. We can make our cells and our aura brighter by reducing obstacles, barriers and conflicts ACMES.

This topic is taken up at length in *Radical Cell Wellness-- Especially for Women!*

Maryann Castellanos has found a useful way to talk about our unresolved sub and unconscious conflicts in a general way. She observes that most of our conflicts are visible as metaphoric "horizontal plates of glass" between the north (cerebral) and south (enteric) poles of our psyche.

Any time we reduce inner barriers and conflicts between north and south in our psyche, we make our aura brighter.

Abundant communication north and south inside our microscopic cells increases their energetic exchange and vitality. The same applies to us as five or six foot tall adults. The more integrated we are top and bottom, the fewer inner barriers we have, the greater our vitality. This topic is usefully discussed as improving coherence between our Inner Court in the gut and our Inner Court in the head, beyond our scope here.

.v\V/v.

NEW Energy Anatomy

Why auras and seven chakras are naturally the tail, not the dog of energy anatomy

Q: What's wrong with the seven chakras?

A: Nothing is wrong with them. What's wrong is how we think about them. Until our schools educate and draw out more than only the intellect, we look at everything expecting it to be a clockwork mechanism run by logic.

We look at a visual of the seven traditional chakras first drawn five thousand years ago—and we see a clockwork. We start imagining—incorrectly—the seven centers work up and down and as a hierarchy. This kind of thinking if for the neck up, for the intellect only. It's the kind of thinking our intellect likes because it's the kind of thinking our intellect can understand.

Our 3D physical body is the after effect, the final out-picturing of all the activity in our inner psyche and consciousness. Our physical-material body devolves and precipitates from all our higher frequency subtle bodies.

A humorous contrast exists here with early nineteenth century material-scientific psychology; it believed the reverse: our psyche was merely an after effect of the physical body!

Lost in the intellectual fantasies the intellect can supply our small "s" ego, is how our seven centers work more like a hologram than as a machine. This idea only entered the mainstream in the 1980s. The clockwork machine assumptions we make about the seven traditional centers are way out of date now.

Given our intellectual education, entering the topic of human energy thru the topic of the seven traditional etheric centers, is throwing a two year old who wants to learn swimming, right into the deep end of the pool.

Our 'habit body' as a 'habit hologram'

The metaphor of a hologram is a good way to pierce thru to the "bigger you" behind the smokescreens in our language and our perceiving. The hologram metaphor helps us reframe the "bigger me," the "bigger you" with new eyes.

Modern people already know a hologram has three dimensions; and yet, its internal structure is significantly non-physical in nature. Therefore, a hologram is more similar, than any other science thing, to how our psyche is structured.

This similarity is no accident! Our psyche is well-described as a hologram of physical, imaginal, emotional, mental and mythological potentials. Some are more activated than others. Some potentials are stuck and require attention.

Michael Talbot's *Holographic Universe: The Revolutionary Theory of Reality* (1984), raised the question, 'How do we apply the metaphor of a hologram to human psychology and self-healing?' The answer was already somewhat obvious to practitioners of both Applied Kinesiology and Touch for Health who were both using muscle testing to explore, measure and assess the unconscious workings of our psyche. AS NLP overlapped with Touch for Health around 1990, the psyche began to look more and more like some kind of living hologram.

Talbot's exploration ran into difficult terrain when he found "...evidence to suggest that our world and everything in it. . . are also only ghostly images,

NEW Energy Anatomy

projections from a level of reality beyond our own..."

Enter another reporter, Lynne McTaggart. In *The Field: The Quest for the Secret Force of the Universe,* she explored aspects of the New Science paradigm, how mind and body are not as separate from each other and the environment as Old Science imagined; but rather, all are part of a "vast energy sea, and that consciousness may be central in shaping our world." McTaggart asserted a "cobweb of energy exchange" links everything in physical Creation.

We can better sequence these two foundational reporting efforts in front of, and as introduction to, the deeper insights gained by Rudolf Steiner and his students from the 1920s thru the 1950s on the topic of "etheric formative forces." Together these make a solid 'ramp of understanding' to understand our psyche as living 3D holograms around and within our physical body. This same language furnishes us understanding of the etheric body, the "web that has no weaver" in acupuncture that unites each of us into individuals who can say, "I am;" and unites all of Creation into one planet, one solar system, one galaxy, one universe, each in turn.

The "bigger me" closest to us, the conscious self, is known by many familiar names: inner child, immune system, and so on. Since the 1990s NLP, New German Medicine and Social Panoramas have projected bright lights into the unconscious enabling us for the first time to see more of the mechanisms of our habit body in motion and at work.

Not everyone is interested in the "bigger you." To perceive our own hologram body, we have to overcome the over-familiarity and lack of precise language; that up to now, has kept our own hologram invisible to us.

We find our own hologram is a highly patterned 'habit hologram' of several levels of living habits:

- Physical habits,

- Imaginal habits,

- Emotional habits,

- Beliefs (mental habits),

- Favorite archetypes and fairy tales we live our lives by.

at various frequencies, have inside us can be understood in terms of a 3D framework and a hologram is the way to "see" this, the structure of the "bigger you."

A full discussion of how the "bigger you" is structured and organized as a hologram, and the history of this idea, in included in this work.

The old approach to the esoteric thru auras and chakras was designed for clairvoyant initiates. It was NOT a step-wise process into the mysteries and wonders of in the human psyche for students of self-healing. The old historical approach was all the original Theosophists had—but since the 1970s we've had 40 years of kinesiology testing and synthesis to make what used to be esoteric-- ordinary and accessible, for those looking for this in a context of loving.

Today, for non-clairvoyant students, it's more practical to start with the hologram metaphor and unambiguous physical and energetic anatomy based on elementary geometry of top~bottom, right~left, front~back. This creates openings for students to find their own reference points and further subtleties themselves.

Our major etheric centers are indeed a ladder, a continuum of frequencies, low to high, as you go up the body HOWEVER this is the tail of the dog—not the dog. They are not PRIMARILY a ladder of frequency. They are

NEW Energy Anatomy

primarily a hologram.

Ask anyone with direct perception of chakras and you hear how intensely personal, unique and difficult to interpret they are. In our chakras and auras we are **least similar** to each other. Our etheric centers are our most subjective dimension, expressing unconscious facets in a personal symbolic language, each person with their own highly evolved language!

Because Auras and chakras remain notoriously subjective and difficult to interpret directly, virtually all books describe them in only very generic ways.

K-testing is the much more precise tool, limited only by the questions you can ask. With it you can talk directly to the immune system, the keeper of the etheric centers and uncover much more of what is "true" for the body and psyche. K-testing will also always suggest how each person heals uniquely, a prime tenet to live by.

Auras and chakras were by the design of Angels to be very far away from the conscious self, a classic example of, "If you had direct hands-on access to them, you would mess it up."

We might wish more detail on our etheric centers, to bring them closer thru clairvoyant observation; however, clairvoyant perception is a tool accessible to few; and, each individual's centers are not very similar close-up to any one else's.

K-testing on the other hand can be learned by anyone wishing to learn. Aligning K-testing with Love, Light and Angels, asking for them to be your partners in every session, increases its utility.

We are most similar to each other in the two poles of our psyche. First, in the shape and functions of our physical body; second, in our soul. In between, in the rest of our psyche, colored as it is by many existences of biography and by our unconscious memories, habits and behaviors, we are more unique than similar. We are similar again at the level of soul.

So if a child wants to swim, do you throw them immediately into the deep end of the swimming pool? No, you let them wade in at the shallow end, get acclimated, and build confidence. Later on, when they are ready, they dive in at the deep end.

The location and frequency of centers is easy to test for—but not the unresolved issues contained therein. Our seven major etheric centers influence our blood, muscle, bones, metabolism and so on. However, the centers are more distant and dissociated energetically from blood, organs, muscles, and bones than casual observers realize.

Carolyn Myss has made a heroic effort in her books to create a psychology of the centers. What's clear now is our centers are actually quite far away and far apart from anything called "psychology" if by "psychology" you mean "makes sense to the rational mind."

Compared to etheric centers, our acupuncture meridians are much higher in the psyche, closer to the sub-conscious, closer to something the sequential mind can grasp.

The we have the 12 meridians and two major vessels. The meridians are much more psychology-friendly and also mythology-friendly. Find a full discussion of the psychology of the 2 vessels and 12 meridians as a "map" and guide to sub- and unconscious disturbances in the human being in *Meridian Metaphors, Psychology of the meridians and major organs* which in part summarizes William Whisenant's 400 page, *Psychological Kinesiology* (1994).

NEW Energy Anatomy

Sadly perhaps, the etheric centers do not lend themselves to this kind of psychological and mythological interpretation. Everyone who has tried this has developed a unique and stand alone system difficult for other people to penetrate and make use of, in my survey of the literature.

The "language" of the centers is very dissimilar from the linear and sequential language of our rational mind. Our thinking mind does NOT have any ability to change them directly, with any long lasting results. See also, "Avoid persons promising to change your centers directly" below.
Q: What about our glands? Do you also downplay the metaphysical interpretation of the glands?
A: No. The meaning of the glands, their under- and overcharge dysfunctions and healthy states are very useful in my practice. This subject is already covered in depth in Meridian Metaphors. In trying to add to this manual, I realized someone with a lot more talent and experience with the glands should be writing this topic, not me!
Q: Is there no good book on the etheric centers?
A: Yes, Richard Jelusich's Eye of the Lotus (2004), the only book on etheric centers I own, a good reference text for practitioners.
Feel free to call for a gift consultation, sign up for the newsletter, attend classes and group consults.

.v\V/v.

About the Author

Bruce co-founded the Holistic Chamber of Commerce in Los Angeles. A trained Waldorf teacher, he's also USM, Peace Theological Seminary, BreakThrough Parenting and NVC-trained. He has seen clients professionally since 2001. He has 15 books/eBooks on Best Practices in Holistic Self-Healing.

Find him at http://www.HealingToolbox.org

NEW Energy Anatomy

Tools That Heal Press booklist

Best Practices in Holistic Self-Healing Series

Resources written by and for self-testers

In all modalities

Tools That Heal composed by and for self-healers and self-muscle-testers in all therapeutic modalities.

HealingToolbox.org ~ *310-280-1176* ~ Gift sessions by phone to find and repair the weak link in your Ring of Success. Practitioners, healers and coaches especially invited to call.

All books written in an interactive, FUN style by a practicing Health Intuitive with training from MSIA, USM, NVC and Waldorf teacher training from Rudolf Steiner College.

All books available in PAPER and EBOOK.

Best Selling titles

Meridian Metaphors, Psychology of the Meridians and Major Organs

Ever wonder what the connection between meridians, organs and emotions is? Ever think TCM had a start on good ideas but much was missing? Now anyone can work either forwards or backwards, between disturbed organs and meridians on one hand; and, disturbed mental-emotional states on the other hand. All descriptions begin with healthy function. Disturbances are further categorized by under- and overcharge conditions. Includes the myths and metaphors of under-overcharged organs-meridians condensed from Psychological Kinesiology plus much new material from other clinical practitioners. 22,000 words 80 page manual, 8 x10".

.c\C/c.

NEW Energy Anatomy

The NEW Energy Anatomy:

Nine new views of human energy that don't require clairvoyance

The Three Selves is simply the clearest, easiest map-model for the whole person. Here's the greater detail you would expect in an anatomy that goes with the 3S.

An easier, simpler, faster way to learn about human energy system compared to the chakra system. The NEW Energy Anatomy is a better entry point for students to developing sensitivity. Each view is testable with kinesiology of any and all kinds. You be the judge!

Physical anatomy is used by every effective energetic practitioner and self-healer. When your target is invisible, as often true--the best map is invaluable!

Maps of chakras, auras, acupuncture points, and reflex points are common—and commonly confusing to students because they cannot be perceived directly without clairvoyance. If you ARE clairvoyant, these aspects are easier to perceive and lead into the even deeper symbology of the chakra system.

These nine simpler views replace the chakra system as a starting place for most students of human energy. Each one is testable with kinesiology of any method. See for yourself!

NEW Energy Anatomy replaces some of the older views of human energy with views much simpler to visualize

Particularly useful for energy school students and sensitive persons using testing to sort out their abundant perceptions. More generally useful for efforts to become more Coherent, Integrated and Aligned (the new CIA). Coupled with Touch for Health, EFT, Energy Medicine or PTS Masters and Doctorate programs, these views facilitate making your aura brighter.

Human energy is organized:

1) Right and left in the body, yin & yang in the body.
2) Top and bottom, enteric and cerebral nervous systems.
3) Front and back, CV-GV, Clark Kent and Superman.
4) As frequency, best viewed as four kinds of laughter!
5) Our gut brain has two frequencies, divided top and bottom, feeling above (hey, hey hey!) and willingness below (ho, ho, ho!).
6) Our inner child has four distinct quadrants, an Inner Court.
7) We have a second Inner Court in our head.
8) The back of our head is willingness to heal our past.
9) Hip stability is a Ring of Loving you can strengthen.

Other material includes the Law of Gentleness for healers, coaches & counselors. 25,000 words 145 p. in 6x9 format.

.c\C/c.

NEW Energy Anatomy

Best Practices in Holistic Self-Healing Series

1) You have FIVE bodies, PACME, Spiritual Geography 101

99 cents. eBook A fundamental distinction John-Roger and others make early and often is the useful tool of Spiritual Geography, discerning we have not one body here on Earth, but FIVE. Take away or compromise with any one of these bodies and we become less than fully human, less than fully capable of giving and receiving love. Topics include:

What makes us human is primarily invisible

Experience your five bodies RIGHT NOW

Two simple spiritual geographies

The map of Creation in your own hand

PACME ~ CIEMU: low frequency to high frequency

Tiger's Fang & When Are You Coming Home?

CIEMU can also be concentric circles

We have habits and comfort zones on each level CIEMU

Can I measure the soul here in 3D?

Can I see the soul here in the 3D world?

How does Spirit view my illness?

Where does physical disease come from?

Where are the primary causative factors of illness?

Only two kinds of problems

Why is the outer world more compelling than the inner?

Redeeming the imagination

.c\C/c.

2) Your Habit Body, An Owner's Manual

Our Habit Body is our best and closest friend. It remembers every routine thing we do daily--so we don't have to relearn all our habits all over again each day. Habits are reactivity set on automatic, behavior conditioned to repeat.

NEW Energy Anatomy

Your Habit Body — An Owner's Manual. A three selves journal. Bruce Dickson, HealingCoach.org

If this is so, how come the one thing human beings do better than anything else is to make the same mistake over and over and over again?

Based on results, we don't know as much about our habit body as people think. We need new Tools That Heal to get at the 90% of our habit body that is sub- and unconscious.

We have habits on five personality levels: physical, imaginal, emotional, mental and unconscious. How are they organized? How do we keep all our habits organized so when we wake up in the morning, we don't have to relearn everything? Personal-spiritual growth is upgrading our habits on any of these levels. Sound like a lot to manage? This makes your job easier, the missing manual for anyone who owns a Habit Body.

We used to say, "He who doesn't know his history is doomed to repeat it." We can say more precisely, "Whoever neglects their habit body will have the same behaviors and results tomorrow, as they did yesterday." Find answers here:

- Why we were more lovable when we were young

- Every day we are "training a new puppy"

- Why 90% of habits are invisible in 3D

- A dozen common terms for the "habit body."

Garrison Keillor says, "Culture is what you know is so by age 12." ALL culture can be seen as just a bunch of habits, including your own. Once you can see it, you can redirect it. 78 pages.

.c\C/c.

3) Self-Healing 101; Nine Experiments in Self-healing

You Can Do at Home to Awaken the Inner Healer

Anyone CAN self-heal. Wherever you are is a good place to start. You can start NOW

For those looking to go deeper into self-healing and/or begin or deepen their practice of self-muscle-testing. Alternatively, for those teaching others how to self-muscle-test.

Self-healing and self-

NEW Energy Anatomy

muscle-testing is outside the exhausted residue of Cartesian-Newtonian Science. Self-healing and self-muscle-testing is really part of the more appropriate newer Goethean Holistic Science; that is, all results, all phenomena, are replicable but NOT by all persons, at all places and all times, regardless of intention. Rather results are replicable primarily in the domain of one person.

Q: How do I begin our own journey of self-healing in the domain of one person, myself?

A: We move to a more experiential approach to self-healing beginning with

- Self-acceptance, self-love

- prayers of self-protection

- self-sensitivity

- self-permission to make testing experiments.

In hands-on Goethean Holistic Science experiments, there is no penalty for failure, none at all--as long--as you learn something from every experiment.

The only wrong way to experiment is not to try at all.

.c\C/c.

4) You are a Hologram Becoming Visible to Your Self

The bigger part of us, our inner child, immune system, high self, "true self," "divine connection"--however you term it, is invisible to us for several reasons--but you can change this and get to know the "bigger you."

The metaphor of a hologram is a good way to see the "bigger you" behind all the familiar smokescreens.

A hologram metaphor assists us to reframe the "bigger you" with new eyes. As modern people, we understand a hologram has both three dimensions and internal structure. These are useful metaphors for our inner dimensions and the structures in our sub- and unconscious. Our psyche is a hologram of physical, imaginal, emotional, mental and mythological potentials. Some are fully activated, many are not. Some are stuck and dysfunctional.

What we have inside us can be understood in terms of a 3D framework and a hologram is the way to "see" this, the structure of the "bigger you."

A full discussion of how the "bigger you" is structured and organized as a hologram, and the history of this idea, in included in this work.

.c\C/c.

NEW Energy Anatomy

5) "Willingness to heal is the pre-requisite for all healing"

This quote from Bertrand Babinet begins exploration and expansion of some of Bertrand Babinet's wonderful legacy of theory and method.

If you can do kinesiology testing by any method, you can measure your own willingness to heal. Self-testers can measure their own willingness to heal, in your inner child.

This tells you if your silent partner is ready to heal what you wish to heal. You can use this to explore where you are most ready to grow.

Have clients? The effectiveness of any energetic session can be estimated AHEAD OF TIME, with surprising accuracy--before you begin working! Practitioners in any and all modalities, are encouraged measure willingness to heal FIRST!

Save your self from wasting effort when clients are of two minds on their issue and do not know this. The higher the number on a scale of 1-10, the more momentum your client has to heal on that issue.

Willingness to heal is the key to aligning and integrating the three selves. Willingness is where the whole topic of the 3S leads.

NOTE ~ This booklet assumes readers can already either self-test using kinesiology testing—K-testing, dowsing, or some other form; or, can follow instructions to use any partner to do two-person testing, termed Client

Controlled Testing. Problems with your own testing? Don't trust your own results? See the training protocol breakthroughs in *Self-Healing 101.*

.c\C/c.

6) You Have Three Selves; Simplest, clearest model of the Whole Person

Volume ONE, Orientation

Compose your own vision of self-healing with the first comprehensive general textbook on the Three Selves. The basic self is functionally equal to the inner child, Little Artist, immune system and 12 other 20th century terms. The conscious self is your rational mind, which can be either feeling or thinking! Your high self is your guardian angel, your own higher Guidance. Aligning all three of these on the

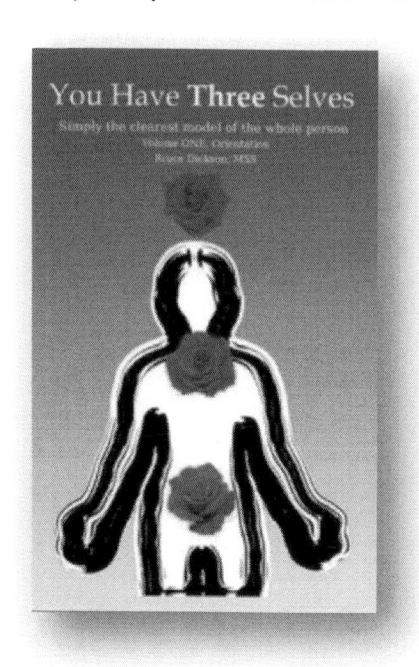

NEW Energy Anatomy

same goal so they can work as a team, describes much of what we do in 3D embodiment. Written with diagrams and much humor. 223 p. 6x9"

.c\C/c.

7) You Have Three Selves; Simplest, clearest model of the Whole Person;

Volume TWO, Finding the 3S in Your Life

If the Three Selves are universal and pervasive in psychology, they ought to be visible all around us. Yikes, it's true! Find the 3S in your body, in pop culture, in the fun of Transactional Analysis, etc. 93 p. 6x9"

.c\C/c.

8) The Inner Court: Close-up of the Habit Body

This is a more exact, body-based, imagination than the "inner child;" also, a moral imagination, disciplining us to see more clearly inside yet NOT spiral up into unbridled fantasy.

The four archetypal characters, Guinevere, Lancelot, Merlin & King Arthur (GLMA) function as starting places to penetrate into your own sub- and unconscious habit body where our habits, behaviors, and comfort zones are all running and repeating. Arthurian legend figures in because all expressions, described in legend are a map, a guide, of possible behaviors and expressions open to us. both functional and dysfunctional. This map of inner child is four times as precise as Bradshaw's unitary concept of the "inner child."

All insights are easily transferred to working with clients. The map does not determine the territory; GLMA do not determine personality. Yet, our virtually every possible like & dislike, strength & weakness, are all "programmed" into the firmware of our Inner Court. Nothing is immutable; it's all habits; if you can access a dysfunctional habit, there is Grace available to redirect,

NEW Energy Anatomy

upgrade, change or release it.

Further, we have TWO Inner Courts, one in our gut brain, a second on in the four brain quadrants. The two Courts make the previously mysterious topics of self-esteem and self-concept understandable.

The greater precision of the Inner Court makes clear the conceptual strengths and weaknesses of Personality Typologies such as MBTI, how personality is formed thru preferences:

- Aristotle-Steiner's four Temperaments and other typologies NOT body-based,

- The wonderful work of Ned Herrmann & Katherine Benziger is clarified and made more artistic,

- The promise of earlier research on Right and left brain blossoms fully in the Inner Court.

- Upgrading the Inner Court is a bridge to widen the bottlenecks of personal-spiritual growth.

The books clearly lists dysfunctional expressions of each member of the Inner Court, providing body-centric maps to locate where everyday disturbances originate and track back to. If you can feel it—and locate it--you can heal it! All aspects of the Inner Court lends itself highly to muscle testing experiments.

The Inner Court model is appropriate to grad students and ANYONE interested in counseling, coaching, training, sales and personal growth. 116 p. 6x9".

.c\C/c.

9) The Five Puberties, a Three Selves Journal on Children

Growing new eyes to see children and stage-development afresh is the goal of this booklet. It builds on the foundation of the other volumes—or--can be read alone. Children are viewed thru lenses not often used: body posture, stories the body tells, animals, plants, the succession of puberties--at least four puberties--each of us undergoes on our journey towards independent thinking.

Finally, we glance at what progress has been made towards a functional typology of children's temperaments in Anthroposophy, MBTI and Katherine Benziger, providing some directions for fruitful further study. The perplexing problem of how children's typology differs from adult typology, is brought close to resolution.

.c\C/c.

NEW Energy Anatomy

10) Radical Cellular Wellness—Especially for Women

Cell psychology for everyone; a coherent theory of illness and wellness.

Finally a Theory of Illness and a Theory of How We Heal for everyone—especially for women: your cells are born healthy; and left on their own, cells remain healthy and reproduce perfectly. It is only environmental and human pollution that interferes with cell health and reproduction.

The various forms of internal pollution we allow, promote and create are discussed with an eye to solutions!

.c\C/c.

Works incidental & complementary to Best Practices Series, above

- The Meaning of Illness is Now an Open Book;

Cross-referencing Illness and Issues

Virtually unknown to the public, EIGHT excellent, peer-reviewed books exist correlating illnesses and mental-emotional issues as of 2013.

It's now possible to simply look up the meaning of physical illnesses, the causative issues behind health concerns. Some combination of these mental-emotional issues is what oppresses your organs, tissues and cells.

For persons with their own Healing Toolbox, they can simply get busy doing what you can to locate, address and resolve these issues. Muscle testing, kinesiology testing of any kind is the most convenient way to navigate to which issue is "live" in you.

NEW Energy Anatomy

If you don't know where your Healing Toolbox is or what's in it, you can always find a Self-Healing Coach, Health Intuitive or Medical Intuitive. Find someone who works with loving.

Those interested in the mental-emotional meaning of illnesses tend to be, self-healers, self-muscle-testers, holistic practitioners, kinesiology practitioners, Medical and Health Intuitives, energy detectives of all kinds and anyone interested in what used to be called "psychosomatic medicine."

Therapeutically useless and eccentric literature in this field does exist. This only highlights the eight best books.

Additional material concerns how one Medical Intuitive views his field and his practice:

- Illness as a healing metaphor.

- Willingness to heal is the pre-requisite to heal

- Summary of some very recent protocols and methods for connecting the dots between illnesses and issues.

Chapter Four has some original research on therapeutic metaphors for illness:

Cancer and tumors in general

Stroke

SIDS

Autism

Alzheimer's

ADHD, Attention deficit, Hyperactive disorder

Chapter Five is a Proposed Wikipedia page upgrade on "Medical Intuitive"

.c\C/c.

- Rudolf Steiner's Fifth Gospel in Story Form

One of the wonderful experiences of my Waldorf teacher training was in a comfy living room, with a group of friends, reading aloud Rudolf Steiner's Fifth Gospel transcripts, round-robin style, a paragraph at a time. We read a chapter each night over the 12 Days of Christmas. If you've done this, maybe you also felt the pull to draw closer to this material. I certainly did.

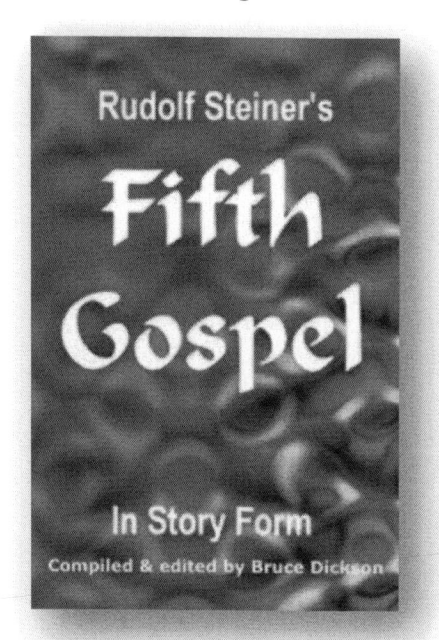

Dr. Steiner's aim was to update the biography of Jesus of Nazareth, in light of the expanded psychological understanding of karma and reincarnation

NEW Energy Anatomy

flourishing in the West between 1880 and 1920.

The imaginative capacity of humankind, our increased ability to process metaphor, demonstrated by Depth Psychology and Carl Jung, made possible this portrait of Jesus of Nazareth and what he transformed into. RS's Fifth Gospel remains the most psychologically astute portrait of Jesus of Nazareth this author is aware of.

An unexpected function of this material is it can support people who have lost the thread of connection with their own internal Christ spark, our immortal-eternal soul. Steiner's Fifth Gospel is an opportunity to pick up the thread of their own connection again. RS's ideas can be very healing to many conventional ideas about Jesus of Nazareth.

What Steiner found in the Akashic Records, regarding the life of Jesus of Nazareth, was a series of "story book images." These are apparently quite closely and faithfully approximated by both children's Sunday School images of the life of Christ; and also by, traditional stained glass windows of the Stations of the Cross.

If you know him, you won't be surprised to hear Steiner dove into and behind these images to penetrate their inner reality; and then, articulate it in modern language for modern minds.

Steiner's verbatim lecture transcripts of his investigations were published in a book called The Fifth Gospel, but his basic clairvoyant research was never compiled nor edited; nor, was any attention paid to building a mood.

Topics include:

Inner experience of the disciples at Pentecost.

The two Jesus children, tradition of and evidence for.

Contribution of the Buddha to the Luke Jesus child.

The shepherds see the astral body of Buddha.

.c\C/c.

- How We Heal; and, Why do we get sick?

Including 35 better, more precise questions on wellness and healing, answered by a Medical Intuitive

Why every illness is a healing metaphor A theory of Cellular Awakening, short version.

Your personal beliefs & myths about healing.

#1: If we understand our problems, they will be healed.

#2: If you don't know and don't understand, then you can't heal.

#3: Personal-spiritual

NEW Energy Anatomy

change takes a long time and is always a slow process. After all, you've had the problem for a long time.

#4: If you've had a negative belief for a long time, it will take a long time to change.

#5: If you change quickly, it must be superficial and not long lasting.

#6: I can't change; "This is the way I am; I'll always be this way."

#7: If you are middle-aged or older, it is too late to change.

#8: Changing old behaviors and thought patterns is often difficult and painful, "No pain, no gain."

Why is pain allowed? Why do I put up with so much pain in my body?

Can you help me see disease from Spirit's point of view?

18 more questions--answered!

.c\C/c.

COMING early 2014: Muscle Testing as a Spiritual Exercise;

Building a Bridge to Your Body's Wisdom

- Muscle-Testing Redesigned for 'God is my Partner'

- How to tune into the "bigger you"

- Making healthier choices is for everyone

The Healing Toolbox approach to "how to do muscle testing."

I began writing this book around 2001. Why the long gestation? Almost the whole modern history of muscle testing had to be stood on its head, everything I had learned from dowsing and then Touch for Health. Conventional approach to muscle testing had to be DIS-connected from Cartesian-Newtonian science; then, plugged into Goethean Holistic Science. Consequently, this is NOT your mother's-father's kinesiology manual.

22 videos are also referenced and their topics are expanded on here.

Our small intestine is already muscle testing 24/7. As waking-conscious selves, we can re-arrange our thinking to use this to our advantage. It requires some lively conceptual ju-jitsu. I believe the journey will be both practical and entertaining.

ANY method on the Skill Ladder of Holistic Self-healing Techniques-Methods-Arts is useful on a Heroes Journey of Self-healing. Cessation of inner againstness and releasing of outworn "stories" PACME is always good.

The Skill Ladder is here: "A clear skill ladder exists of holistic self-healing methods-techniques-arts"

NEW Energy Anatomy

http://www.healingtoolbox.org/k2-stub/item/333-skill-ladder-of-holistic-healing-methods-techniques-arts

This book address primarily only the technique-method-art of self-muscle-testing.

Arm-length-testing is preferred for beginners over all other methods. Any other method of muscle testing is fine too. Arm-length-testing is here: http://innerwise.com/en/videos/all-videos/113-innerwise-the-arm-lenght-test?category_id=54COMING: Best Practices in Holistic Self-Healing Series

.c\C/c.

COMING early 2014:

Measuring, math and scales--with 'God as my Partner

Many Goethean Science experiments in self-testing to explore, experiment and expand skills in self-healing. Written for dowsers, self-testers, self-healers and those wishing to improve their self-testing.

ALL exercises here REQUIRE familiarity and/or some skill with muscle testing, kinesiology testing, dowsing.

If you like and dislike things, you are already measuring invisible--still real things. Every time you choose one option over another, you are measuring invisibles.

You measure if the weather is too hot or too cold to wear this or that clothing. If you sing, you are constantly measuring to stay on key. If you dance, you are constantly measuring if your are following the rhythm or not. All these things are invisible.

May as well get good at measuring invisibles, we do it every day.

When we add scales and numbers to our unconscious measuring exercises, we include, train and strengthen the conscious-waking self.

With children, after age seven, to support their conscious self, we encourage accurate counting of physical items via math manipulatives.

For adults, counting invisible things precisely is mostly called "muscle testing," sometimes "dowsing." Muscle testing of any kind strengthens the conscious self even more quickly than math manipulatives because we are attending to real things that while unseen, are still countable.

The healthy human being is the primary and sometimes only accurate measuring tool for measuring character, as we do in voting, elections and mate selection. May as well get good at it!

.c\C/c.

Holistic Chamber Start-up Kit (2009 edition)

NEW Energy Anatomy

Everything you need to start your own local Holistic Chamber of Commerce .A fundraiser for local HCCs everywhere!

Each copy purchased benefits the local Chamber you buy it from. Bruce Dickson, Founder, Co-Chair ToolsThatHeal.com ~ HealingCoach.org

Camille Leon, Co-Chair ~ Westside Holistic Chamber of Commerce & http://www.holisticchamberofcommerce.com

8,000 words to inspire you to start a local chamber, where the network is, tips and hard-won experience to save you time on the front end. Concludes with some ideas you can implement once you get going.

Connect with the Author ~

Find Bruce at http://www.HealingToolbox.org

Gift initial sessions available for a while longer.

Bruce has a series of 15 books, 20 videos and the Inner Dashboard method.

Sessions with the author

Gift initial sessions available for a while longer. Between 8:00 am and 9:00 pm PST.

HealingToolbox@gmail.com Skype: SelfHealingCoach

Health Intuitive Bruce Dickson shows people how to use their own Inner Dashboard so they can increase their own Inner Sunshine. How? By identifying and removing blocks and obstacles to inner Light & Sound.

With your permission, Bruce talks directly with your immune system and your own Guidance, to learn what's oppressing your cells. He shows you how to throw off burdens you no longer wish to carry.

"Working from my own limited mind is inefficient and not much fun. It works better to work from your own higher Guidance. Your Benefactors know you better than I; they know the path to your next healing better than I, so I let them lead."

Want homework? Many ways to connect with your own Guidance exist thru the Skill Ladder of Holistic Self-healing Techniques-Methods-Arts.

Let's all use more Tools That Heal and apply Best Practices in Self-Healing; including, Slow-Motion Forgiveness(SM).

$45 for 30 mins. $80 hour. Money-back guarantee on all work.

NEW Energy Anatomy

Training with the Author

If you can't go backwards

and can't remain where you are,

I encourage you to begin your own Heroes journey of self-healing.

If you are a holistic practitioner looking for more Tools That Heal and/or develop your own system, let's talk. Video class in the works.

Between 8:00 am and 9:00 pm PST.

HealingToolbox@gmail.com Skype: SelfHealingCoach

$45 for 30 mins. $80 hour.

Other products

Slow-Motion Forgiveness ™ Practice CD

The Five Puberties, a 3S journal on Children, 40 p. 6x9"

The Meaning of Illness Is Now an Open Book, Free 31 page PDF by request.

Muscle Testing Practice Group DVD. One hour.

1:1 phone sessions available. Group classes available. Training to do what I do is available.

HealingToolbox.org

Reading Group Guide

Best Selling titles:

Meridian Metaphors, Psychology of the Meridians and Major Organs

The NEW Energy Anatomy: Nine new views of human energy; No clairvoyance required

Best Practices in Holistic Self-Healing Series

1) You have FIVE bodies PACME; Spiritual Geography 101

2) Your Habit Body, An Owner's Manual Our habits are our best friends; why then, do we make the same errors over and over again?

3) Self-Healing 101; Nine Experiments in Self-healing, You Can Do at Home to Awaken the Inner Healer

4) You are a Hologram becoming visible to yourself

5) "Willingness to heal is the pre-requisite for all healing"

6) You Have Three Selves Vol ONE; Simply the clearest model of the whole person; Orientation

7) You Have Three Selves; Vol TWO; Find the 3S in your life & pop culture

8) The Inner Court: Close-up of the Habit Body

NEW Energy Anatomy

9) The Five Puberties, Growing new eyes to see children afresh

10) Radical Cell Wellness—Especially for women! Cell psychology for everyone; A coherent theory of illness and wellness

Works incidental-complementary to Best Practices series, above

- The Meaning of Illness is Now an Open Book, Cross-referencing illness and issues

- How We Heal; and, Why do we get sick? Including 35 better, more precise questions on wellness and healing, answered by a Medical Intuitive

- Rudolf Steiner's Fifth Gospel in Story Form Topics include the TWO Jesus children and the active participation of the Buddha in the Christ event.

Other CLASSICS of self-healing & Medical Intuition

MSIA Discourses
http://www.msia.org/discourses

Forgiveness, Key to the Kingdom, John-Roger

The Emotion Code, Bradley

Nelson

Messages From the Body, Michael Lincoln

Our Many Selves, Elizabeth O'Connor

Touch for Health, 2nd Ed, Mathew Thie

Your Body Speaks Your Mind, 2nd ed. Deb Shapiro

Core Transformation, Connierae Andreas

The best solution is always loving

Did you enjoy this? Please share.

If you get stuck, give me a call.

What if a fraction of the new replacement culture, you and I are creating now, will begin around self-healing and training activity as the cultural benefit of the hard work of building new, sustainable, intentional community?